Elvis Costello
This Year's Model

Laura Shenton

"My songs have to do with situations. They aren't philosophical treatises. I didn't name the songs 'guilt', 'revenge', or 'sarcasm'. The journalists did that."

- Elvis Costello, as quoted in *Crawdaddy* in March 1978

Elvis Costello
THIS YEAR'S MODEL

Laura Shenton

WYMER
PUBLISHING
Bedford, England

First published in 2021 by Wymer Publishing
Bedford, England www.wymerpublishing.co.uk Tel: 01234 326691
Wymer Publishing is a trading name of Wymer (UK) Ltd

Copyright © 2021 Laura Shenton / Wymer Publishing.

ISBN: 978-1-912782-69-7 (also available as Kindle eBook).

Edited by Jerry Bloom.

The Author hereby asserts his rights to be identified
as the author of this work in accordance with sections
77 to 78 of the Copyright, Designs & Patents Act 1988.

All rights reserved. No part of this publication may be
reproduced or transmitted in any form or by any means,
electronic or mechanical, including photocopying, or any
information storage and retrieval system, without written
permission from the publisher.

This publication is sold subject to the condition that it shall not,
by way of trade or otherwise, be lent, re-sold, hired out or
otherwise circulated without the publishers' prior consent in any
form of binding or cover other than that in which it is published
and without a similar condition including this condition
being imposed on the subsequent purchaser.

Printed and bound in Great Britain by
CMP, Dorset.

A catalogue record for this book is available from the British Library.

Typeset by Andy Bishop / 1016 Sarpsborg.
Cover design by 1016 Sarpsborg.
Cover photo © PictorialPressLtd/AlamyStockPhoto.

Contents

Preface	7
Chapter One: *Why This Year's Model?*	9
Chapter Two: *The Making Of This Year's Model*	33
Chapter Three: *Touring*	51
Chapter Four: *The Legacy*	77
A Comprehensive Discography	103
Tour Dates	107

Preface

Elvis Costello! What a fantastic musician! I trust that you will share such bias with me in reading this book. There is so much to say about him in terms of his unique contribution to music. The purpose of this book is to offer an objective insight into Costello's 1978 album — *This Year's Model* — in terms of the music and the fascinating journey surrounding it. There were so many highs and lows worth documenting including boisterous gigs and ongoing questions surrounding whether or not Costello (born Declan Patrick MacManus) was deliberately trying to shake things up. And that's before the music comes into the picture!

In the interests of transparency and context, as author of this book I have no affiliation with Elvis Costello and I have no affiliation with any of his associates. The content of this book is derived from extensive research fuelled by a passion for his amazing music as well as the hoarding of a range of vintage articles. On such basis, if you're looking for a book that's full of intensely detailed information on someone's personal life, you won't find that here (check out Costello's 2015 autobiography for all that good stuff). This book is the product of an abundance of research and it certainly feels right to collate that here in order to offer an angle on the album that many consider to be Costello's masterpiece.

Notably, When *This Year's Model* was at the peak of its commercial success, many journalists struggled to get an interview with Costello, so much so that in instances where it did happen, the interviewers made specific reference to how pleased they were to finally get to talk to the man in question. Was Costello trying to avoid playing the fame game or was he simply working it all to his own advantage? Read on and form your own opinion. Overall, I am keen to present what happened without painting my own bias on top of it.

This book is a gossip free zone. I want to present facts rather than all kinds of weird and wonderful speculations. Also, there will

Elvis Costello - *This Year's Model*: In-depth

be nothing herein that is in the lexicon of "this song is in B minor so it probably means XYZ." Nope! Not happening! I want to present how the music resonated with people at the time and not what my perception of it is as one of millions of fans out there. Oh, and that reminds me, I was born in 1988 — so ages after all of this stuff happened and thus, this book is a culmination of extensive research that I intend to use objectively to offer a worthwhile narrative on, what is ultimately a very relevant album in *This Year's Model*.

Chapter One
Why This Year's Model?

In 1978, *This Year's Model* was a big deal, not only as a mark of success for Elvis Costello and The Attractions, but in terms of how it was a significant album for the year overall. In December 1978, *Melody Maker* gave it the accolade of Album Of The Year based on the following: "Returning briefly to our original review of Elvis Costello's *This Year's Model* (in March), we find it modestly acclaimed as 'an achievement so comprehensive, so inspired, that it exhausts superlatives... it promotes its author to the foremost ranks of contemporary rock writers.' Familiar, even predictable, hyperbole, perhaps; but on this occasion, at least, such enthusiasm is surely vindicated by the record's decisive musical impact and its powerful resonance. *My Aim Is True*, Costello's 1977 debut, had suggested the emergence of a determinedly individual talent, impatient for success and recognition; a nascent iconoclast ruthlessly dedicated to the notion of unsettling and disturbing the preconceptions of anticipations of his audience with songs of such an explicit emotional force that they often assumed the perverse grandeur of violent personal exorcism. *This Year's Model* transcended the promise of that debut. A superior production — brilliantly streamlined and full of pertinent incident, where its predecessor sounded muted, and, in retrospect, quite conservative — brought into an occasionally blinding focus the complete panorama of Costello's fierce obsessions. The inherent drama of his compositions was similarly underlined with terrific emphasis by the collective performance of his musicians, The Attractions, whose playing captured exactly the neurotic impulse of his songs (Steve Nieve's chilling keyboard interpolations, often approximating icy sound collages, provided an especially appropriate musical backdrop)."

The feature continued, "The entire album betrayed without

Elvis Costello - *This Year's Model*: In-depth

apology Costello's certain knowledge of his own talent: the songs would seem to have been conceived with a confidence that bordered often upon arrogance. Costello, here, seemed to confront with a savage relish both private and universal anxieties. Rarely, it appears, has a performer sought so eagerly to liberate and give voice to every aspect of his complex, often gratuitously provocative, emotional personality. 'Lipstick Vogue', perhaps the most memorable song in his repertoire, is possibly one of the most viciously spiteful songs in the history of rock, and Elvis retreats not an inch from the most forceful expression available to him of its virulent outrage. It's a measure of Costello's sure grasp of both his own anger and frustration and musical dynamics that such typical statements as 'Lipstick Vogue' and, say, 'Lip Service', never descend into mere petulance; the consistency and authenticity of his passion successfully denies such a charge. Furthermore, the penetration of the language of these songs (which literally bristle with inventive and striking juxtapositions of imagery) matches easily the mounting emotional tension. Costello's best songs don't merely evoke or suggest a feeling — he has that rare ability to actually catapult the listener into the kind of turmoil he usually seeks to illustrate (who could listen with any indifference to 'Living In Paradise'?). And, if his work is utterly contemporary in its prickly exposition of hypocrisy — public and personal hypocrisies are relentlessly exposed in those songs — it is not entirely without compassion or concern. 'This Year's Girl' is less an expression of a misogynist temperament than an acute investigation of that mentality; and the haunting 'Night Rally' is an obvious declaration of a more overtly political threat. Elvis Costello may never produce another album as complete in its particular significance as *This Year's Model*, but clearly much of the excitement and exhilaration of the next year will be derived from watching him try."

Despite the commercial success of *This Year's Model*, there was a strong sense that Costello was his own man when it came to the fame game; that is to say that perhaps — to a point — he refused to play it. He was quoted in *New Musical Express* in March 1978; "I don't want to go to lunch with the *Top Of The Pops* producer. People in this fuckin' business just don't understand that I don't want to join their little club. I don't want to go down to the Roxy and hang out with Linda Ronstadt! See, the music-biz as a whole — the crassness

Why This Year's Model?

of it all — still actively disgusts me and any degree of success I may attain will not weigh against all that crap I went through initially. Even if I got to be as big as Fleetwood Mac, I still wouldn't feel any different. But at the same time I don't want to sound obsessed about it, like Phil Spector. Y'know 'people are persecuting me.' Like, I don't think anyone is persecuting me."

In a way, this makes *This Year's Model* all the more fascinating in terms of how, at least as far as his public persona, Costello presented something of a "take it or leave it" attitude with his music. Ironically perhaps, whether he wanted to play the fame game or not, 1978 was a massive year for Elvis Costello and his career. In their end of year summary, *New Musical Express* accounted of Costello in December 1978; "Elvis Costello enthralled, infuriated, intrigued, irritated and got into lots of backstage fights. With two smashes out of three singles ('Chelsea' and 'Radio, Radio' seduced the mass ear, while 'Pump It Up' didn't) and a single success with his *This Year's Model* album, the man who did for horn-rimmed glasses what Elton John did for hair transplants — also achieved the dubious honour of being the first New Wave(ish) artist to have one of his songs recorded by Linda Ronstadt."

It has been the case that Costello's earlier albums — particularly his first two — have been categorised sometimes as punk, sometimes as New Wave. Of course, the two categories both have similarities and differences and a definitive definition is something that could be argued extensively over with still no conclusion drawn. On such basis, it would seem futile to offer a definitive opinion in this book; is *This Year's Model* punk or New Wave? Or indeed, both? Frankly it's too subjective to say. On such basis, the terms are likely to appear interchangeably throughout this book depending on context of what else is being accounted for. Costello said in *Audio Scene Canada* in July 1978; "I never let it bother me that I was being categorised as a punk rock musician. I've learned that there are people who don't know very much about music and need to have their performers put into categories because it's easier for them to understand. Because I don't have respect for people who don't know about music, I don't pay attention to what categories I'm put into."

The following article reflects the extent to which people were really struggling to categorise some styles of music at the time. There

Elvis Costello - *This Year's Model*: In-depth

is a lot to be said for not seeking to label and pigeonhole any art form, but all the same, it is what some people preferred to do. Besides, although the terms that the article was advocating for never took off, it provides an insight into what else was going on in music around the time that Costello was enjoying the success of *This Year's Model*.

Although the majority of the New Wave music emanated from the UK, there was also a movement in the States and this was summed up in an American publication in November 1978. The *Columbia Daily Spectator* offered a summary on what it referred to as "the new High Energy Music and the renaissance of rock and roll"; "When it started, no one knew what to call it. They hit upon the name of punk rock. The promoters of that term were staunch believers in the erroneous assumption that this music was a working class movement. The name changed and the music progressed. New wave they called it. But that wasn't quite true either — you see, how could you call The Rolling Stones and The Who New Wave, when they were such landmarks in the old wave? (Even Bruce Springsteen considers himself a member of this musical form). Then producers just decided to fuck the whole idea and call it what it sounds like. Rock and roll. That's fine, but I prefer high energy music, or even high energy rock and roll. High energy, because that is the most dominant and visible part of the music. Rock and roll, 'cause most of the music is a throwback to the late fifties/early sixties musical genre. Short, powerful songs on relevant topics. Now that we've got a name, how about some sort of idea of what the music is all about? (I hate rhetorical questions, don't you?) High energy music is first of all high in what might be called EQ, or energy quotient. A good way to get an idea of what I'm saying might be to imagine Patti Smith singing 'Rock 'n' Roll Nigger', and then picture the Bee Gees singing about the night fever. If you can do this, you've pretty well got both ends of the scale. The people who play HEM (high energy music) maintain a level of intensity unparalleled in any other musical form. This does not mean that the music is loud. Or rather, that it must be loud. Music does not have to be played any louder than one would play a symphony if the music is high energy. The energy is an intrinsic quality. There are, of course, groups like the Ramones who play their stuff really loud when it would be good at a lower volume. But there are many more groups like the Dead Boys who play their music so that you go home and can't hear for two days in hopes that you won't notice that there's nothing there. Patti Smith does not play her music very loudly, and she is the undisputed priestess of the art."

The feature also argued that the function of HEM was not solely to get you up and boppin', but to offer a kind of music with an essential honesty to it that had not been overproduced. It cited examples of this as The Cars' most recent album at the time, as well as Iggy Pop. Other artists mentioned included Willie Alexander and The Boom Boom Band, Blondie, Talking Heads and Elvis Costello.

In fact, the article concurred that Costello and Patti Smith were the two most talented performers in the realm of HEM. With regard to this very unique English performer, the feature purported, "Costello sings that he 'don't wanna be a goody-goody.' This is the attitude that he presents to audiences. He comes on as someone who is not quite all there, slightly evil but totally honest about what he is and what he wants. It's almost as if he's a disinterested observer of his own life, and, indeed, in many of his songs he is just that. Costello sings about real things and real people. His songs are alive and rough. One can only hope that they don't overproduce him on future albums."

So where did Costello fit into all of this? It was advocated in *Creem* in May 1978; "This acidic, uncompromising musical vision is more reminiscent of classic sixties British club rock than Elvis' New Wave peers. Nevertheless, punk casts a giant shadow over the fiery singer's frantic rock dynamics. The punks grew up under the spell of Iggy and the NY Dolls, Elvis under their equally inspiring antecedents. He reveres rockabilly legends like his namesake and Jerry Lee Lewis, who preferred burning down a stage rather than giving it up; and the original British working class heroes like Arthur Seaton and Jimmy Porter, who bloodied their adversaries in Saturday night pub brawls and stuffed stolen money down drain pipes on Sunday morning. Elvis fits snugly into the new angry young man tradition, soldering a growing distrust of celebrity status to a brash dismissal of sophisticated rock technique and technology. The Ramones practice the put-on, the Pistols preached nihilism. Elvis 'used to be disgusted, now I try to be amused,' striking a delicate balance between the punk party line of parody and pessimism. 'Music is a matter of life and death,' he growled, 'and it doesn't matter at all'."

It was considered in *New Musical Express* in March 1978;

Elvis Costello - *This Year's Model*: In-depth

"Costello can reach people who'd never understand The Clash in a million years. He's capable of getting as big as Elton and Frampton and Fleetwood Mac and The Bee Gees (in case you haven't noticed, it's the Brothers Gibb's turn to be the biggest act in the history of the universe... for this month, anyway) without having to compromise his music by one iota. Like Dylan or Bowie or Neil Young."

Elvis Costello was propelled to fame with the release of his first album, *My Aim Is True*. Combined with a strong stage presence and tight musicianship, things were looking good. The release of his second album, *This Year's Model*, quashed any doubts that Costello was a deserving talent with original ideas and excellent songwriting capabilities.

Released in March 1978, *This Year's Model* got to number four in the UK where it spawned the singles, '(I Don't Want To Go To) Chelsea' which got to number sixteen, 'Pump It Up' which got to number twenty four, and 'Radio, Radio' which got to number twenty nine. In the US, *This Year's Model* went into the top thirty.

Over the spring and summer months of 1978 (see the tour info in the back of this book for dates) Elvis and The Attractions toured the US and Canada. They sometimes shared the bill with Dave Edmunds' Rockpile. The show at the El Mocambo club in Toronto, Canada, was recorded for radio broadcast and was only available in Canada as promotional material. It wasn't long after that it was swiftly released on vinyl as a bootleg. It wasn't until 1993 that the recording would see an official release as part of the boxset, *2½ Years*. It remained the only official live album release of Elvis Costello prior to the 1995 mini album, *Deep Dead Blue* and in 2006, *My Flame Burns Blue*. Back in 1978, the most accessible way for people to hear Elvis Costello and The Attractions was on their recorded work and certainly, *This Year's Model* is a fascinating listen full of social commentary that documents an interesting period in British culture.

Costello rose to fame during a time when the supergroups of the seventies were struggling to garner interest in the mainstream. Bands such as Pink Floyd and Led Zeppelin were no longer seen as cutting edge — by then it was the territory of the likes of the Sex Pistols and the Buzzcocks (at least in terms of the music press and youth culture). As part of this, overall, rock songs about abstract fantasy worlds were on their way out as the youth of Britain were seemingly drawn towards commentaries that had something angry and scathing to say about the conservative mentality of British politics at the time (it wasn't until 1979 that Margaret Thatcher was elected as Prime Minister but even by the late seventies, youth and popular culture embodied a strong anti-establishment narrative via the likes of the Sex Pistols hit, 'God Save The Queen'). With the stage set for wilful rebellion, Elvis Costello certainly wasn't the only young Brit with an axe to grind but above that, his lyrics had bite; they were unapologetically witty. Across a range of relevant subjects, he went beyond complaining about the queen's "fascist regime".

Costello said in *New Musical Express* in March 1978; "I never wanted to be simply one-dimensional, or two-dimensional, for that matter. But you've got to make a stand and go to some extreme in order to establish something directly opposed to all that awful blandness out there. Otherwise you're just another face, another number, so the fact that it's really extreme. I wasn't faking it at all, mind, but still it was right on that very hazy borderline of this whole professional/personal thing where I could've become like the Pistols who stated something totally unacceptable, who cut through everything and ended up cutting their own throats in the process and burying themselves. Just to make that stand, y'know. Personally I'm still not quite sure. There's certainly a lot of strange things going on in my head, a lot of strange things still happening."

Still though, Costello told *Creem* in February 1978; "See I'm twenty two — that's only one year older than Johnny Rotten, isn't it. I just don't want to become the 'elder statesman of punk' or whatever, which is just what Townshend got locked into back in the sixties. It's a dangerous position."

Costello was quoted in the *Bastrop County Times* in July 1978; "We don't want to be trapped in the sort of thirty-five-year-old market. We're trying to break into the younger kind of area."

"The Pistols were the best band to ever come out of England," he told *Creem* in May 1978. "Most groups just destroy themselves when they get on record labels. Look at The Rolling Stones — they've just hung around too long. That's why the Pistols are the best, they haven't stayed beyond their time. Fleetwood Mac — uugghh! They're the dullest group around. Just a washed up old blues group, not challenging at all. They're just safe and convenient to play over and over again. But then, that's America for you... you know there aren't any good American rock bands. You've never contributed one good band to the world... Anyway, where are you going to hear all these great American groups? Not on American radio. It's disgusting that you have so many radio stations and they're all so terrible."

Many were keen to credit Costello for his no-frills approach to rock music. His songs were short and to-the-point with pretty standard instrumentation; bass, guitars, organ, drums and vocals. With his dress sense harking back to the fifties, glasses a la Buddy Holly and slicked back hair, in some ways Costello came across as an underdog; an anti-hero. Added to that, his unique vocal style certainly separated him and his music from the crowd. He explained to *Rock Around The World* in February 1978; "My approach to music is different in that I pick up things that are new and not accepted in hip, critical terms. I don't like a lot of the shouters aspect of entertainment. I think that's a phoney emotion that's sold to people. But then people are basically phoney anyway."

As endearingly eccentric as Costello's public image was, behind all of that, it comes across that in his lyrics, there was a very real anger present with a refreshing degree of frankness. Image aside though, it does come across that Costello was in it for the music.

In *Crawdaddy* in March 1978 he said; "I'm not an artist. Even the word musician I kind of balk at. I'm a songwriter, and I'm a singer. But no hyphen, see? Don't make that mistake. Even a simple mistake like that can be costly in terms of misinformation... What I do is a matter of life and death to me. I don't choose to explain it, of course. I'm doing it, and I'll keep doing it until somebody stops me forcibly."

And in *Circus* in February 1978; "There's nothing glamorous about the world right now, there is no place for glamour or romance... I just don't care about a lot of things; making records, writing songs, and performing is about all. I'm totally serious about what I'm doing, but that doesn't mean there isn't an element of fun involved. I don't want to be so successful that I'll make a lot of money and retire... I'm just interested in playing."

And in *Melody Maker* in May 1978; "I don't want to be successful so that I can get a lot of money and retire to a house in the country. I don't want any of that rock and roll rubbish. I don't want to go cruising in Hollywood or hang out at all the star parties. It's the arse end of rock and roll. I'm just interested in playing music."

The music press perhaps didn't know quite what to make of Elvis Costello. One of his earliest encounters with them was one in which he apparently referred to a "little black book" — a list with the names in of everyone who he felt had wronged him at some point. It was reported that Costello was drunk on Pernod when he slurred this information across to the journalist. Costello had experienced his fair share of rejection prior to getting his big break. He had already sent tapes to several major record companies to no avail. He was from a working class background divided by divorce, but, by several accounts, he wasn't poor or hungry. In such regard, the media at the time sometimes attributed elements of his background in line with his angry image but on other occasions it was put across that his apparent anger was unjustified on the basis that, after all, hadn't many successful musicians been through the wringer before getting their big break?

In June 1978, Nick Lowe said in *Circus* of the time that Costello was struggling to score a record deal; "He's very bitter and twisted about it. He had to go around making a prop of himself in people's offices. I mean, going around playing his songs to people who know nothing about music, people who took one look and thought, 'This guy, I can't sell this bloke'."

Regarding Costello, Columbia A&R Director Gregg Geller told *Circus* in June 1978; "He's a very young, unassuming, talented person who's still learning how to handle all this attention. We certainly succeeded in creating a kind of mystique about him, and since he responds to audience response at his best shows, he tends to taunt them. He can be kind of pleasantly antagonistic."

Lowe said in *Crawdaddy* in July 1978; "I met Elvis at a Brinsleys gig at The Grapes, across the street from The Cavern in Liverpool. I'd seem him at a few gigs, and he asked me something or other. He's always been quiet, I don't know too much about him, really. He tried hard to get a record deal and had a lot of doors slammed in his face. He used to come down and sleep on my floor when he would come down to London. I knew he could play guitar a bit, but he never used to play me any of his songs or anything. Later, he got a group together, but he was always much better than the group. It wasn't until I heard his stuff a few years later, just him and acoustic guitar, that I liked it. He's always very polite to me."

Regardless of what it was that made Elvis Costello angry and whether it was indeed truth or an image exaggerated by both the man himself and the press, it was certainly the case that the anger in the music was undeniable. With driving, relentless rhythms carrying complex and cynical lyrics, Costello's music got through to a wide audience. Another key point about Costello's public image at the time is the fact that he was keen to keep his private life private. It was known that he was born in London and grew up in Liverpool and that he was married with a wife and child but beyond the basics of such statistics, little else was revealed.

Costello was quoted in *Rock Around The World* in February 1978; "With press interviews you're at the mercy of the writer to quote you correctly. That's the main reason I don't like doing press interviews. The reason I don't talk about the past is that I feel it's boring. I don't see any point in drawing upon uninteresting things. The things I find exciting are what I'm doing now and what I'll be doing in the future. To talk about anything else seems to be pointless."

It was reported in *Audio Scene Canada* in July 1978; "Elvis opens up the most when it comes to his music. In particular, he singles out two favourite songs: 'Watching The Detectives' from the first album and 'Radio, Radio' from the *This Year's Model* second album."

In response to the question of whether being a celebrity complicated things for him, Costello said to *Creem* in May 1978; "Bollocks. I'm no celebrity. That's the problem with being a star. You always let people down in the end. I'm not a bloody arbitrator of public opinion. There's no mass following waiting for my next word off the mountain. People should be waiting for their own next word, not mine. Even the money's irrelevant. It's all a matter of whether you own the money or whether the money owns you."

It was reported in *Circus* in June 1978; "Elvis' reclusive nature has kept biographical details scant. Said to have been born in London as Declan Patrick MacManus, raised in Liverpool as a Catholic, Costello is twenty-three, and has a son, three, from a marriage at the age of nineteen. Shortly before his discovery and subsequent induction into the star-making machinery of Columbia Records, Costello was still working as a computer operator at a division of Elizabeth Arden Cosmetics. For a spell, as D.P. Costello, Elvis fronted a country-rocking band called Flip City (his father, as the story goes, was a band-leader). In a boozy interview with a British writer, Costello made a statement that has caused more than a ripple of interest in his way-overgrown cult: 'The only two things that matter to me, the only motivation points for writing these songs, are revenge and guilt.' *This Year's Model* reflects that."

It was considered in *Circus* in February 1978; "Not much is known about Elvis Costello's past and he prefers to keep it that way." To which the singer said, "I'm not particularly proud about what happened before. It's not worth the trouble of going back to look at. I don't see any point in discussing the past. As far as I'm concerned, it's pointless. I'd just rather talk about the future."

In *Creem* in February 1978 he said; "I don't take drugs. I mean, I can't even be in the same room as other people doing cocaine because just being in contact with them, I get three times as wired as them just being there. But I do know what it's like being out of control. I know all about alcohol, for example, because well, let's say I went through my phase of drinking heavily. Really heavily."

Punk and New Wave, by some, were considered to be whole movements — not just in terms of the music but with regards to the fashions, attitudes, and indeed lifestyles that they embodied. By 1978, the pogo dancing and aggression of the rock scene was a world away from the more carefully refined approaches embraced by the likes of Yes, ELP and Jethro Tull. So much so that the record companies were apparently reluctant to sign new acts due to the music scene as a whole being in some kind of limbo between what was no longer fashionable and what was feared to be a fad. Either way, a sense of limbo is fertile ground for something new to come along.

In such regard, it is understandable as to how Punk and New Wave smashed into the mainstream in a big way in the late seventies. A lot of people had grown bored of supergroups and saw them as safe, boring and predictable institutions that didn't speak to the social consciousness anymore.

Costello said in *Creem* in May 1978; "What annoys me the most, is these big bands like Zeppelin and ELP who whine so much about how bad radio is in England, but then they refuse to put out any singles."

Elvis Costello - *This Year's Model*: In-depth

He told *Rock Around The World* in February 1978; "Everybody complains about the state of the music market being filled with disco and the Eagles but they refuse to try and do anything about it unless it involves a compromise. People have become obsessed with making rock and roll something special but it isn't. Rock and roll is the lowest form of life known to man."

Probably not keen to see the status and accessibility of rock 'n' roll being overstated and turned into something disproportionately elusive, Costello said in *Melody Maker* in May 1978; "Too much rock has cut itself off from the people. Its become like ballet or something. Ballet is only for people who can afford to go and see it. It's not for anybody else. You don't get ballet going on in your local pub. There's a lot of rock music that's become exclusive and it's of no use to anyone. Least of all *me*. Music has to get to people. In the heart, in the head. I don't care where as long as it gets them. So much music gets thrown away. It's such a waste."

It was considered in *It's Only Rock 'N' Roll* in May 1978; "Until a couple of years ago, rock 'n' roll was in a death throe. However, with the coming of the New Wave (which some still categorise as punk), new faces, new names, new blood and new life was injected into the lethargic seventies music scene. Armed with aggressive energy, simpler creativity and imagination, a danceable beat (not disco) and a loathing for the overpaid, overly-produced and overly technical groups controlling the state of the art, the New Wavers set out to stand the music world on its brass ear. With the aid of some small record labels such as Stiff, Sire and Beserkley among others, the New Wave bands (mostly from England and New York) reached many an ear. However, it was mainly the ones whose attention had already been captured that they won over. The New Wavers didn't want to destroy the musical structure so much as they wanted to shake it up a bit by integrating and cutting out the fat in order to make rock a lean, viable force once more."

Costello spoke to *Rock Around The World* in February 1978; "I like to think of my music as being of the moment. Throughout the history of popular music, the best of it has been that way. Once an inventive style stops and decides it wants to set itself up as a culture, I think it begins to get boring. What's been missing in music since 1967 is that kind of immediate feeling. Now people are trying to make it into art which it isn't. People are being put to sleep by the excess of most of today's music and the only hope for the form is for musicians and songwriters to bring the music back to the land of the living."

A bold statement but certainly one fuelled by passion and an enthusiasm to break from the same old, same old.

In terms of what *This Year's Model* meant for Elvis Costello's career, the full scale of things becomes apparent when taking the formative years of said career into account. It was reported in *Circus* in February 1978; "A rumour persists that Elvis was a member of the pre-Johnny Rotten Sex Pistols for a brief time, but the only thing you'll get him to admit is that, as recently as last spring, he was a computer analyst in the town of Acton. He had been submitting demos to record companies for over a year before Dave Robinson and Jake Riviera had the foresight to sign him to Stiff Records for a tape recorder and an amplifier. Elvis was not after a big advance, just an opportunity." To which the latter was quoted, "I don't want to spend my time ligging (free-loading) around record company offices like a lot of other musicians. I don't want any charity. I just want to be out gigging and earning money."

Costello got his big break when he responded to an advert placed in the music press. It was placed by one such small and brand new label, Stiff Records. After seeing the advert, Costello took his previously rejected demo tape to the listed address that very same afternoon (hold onto the fact that this was back in August 1976, although Costello rose to success relatively quickly, there was still a lot that went on behind the scenes prior to him becoming a household name).

Stiff Records was the brainchild of Dave Robinson (manager of Graham Parker and The Rumour) and Jake Riviera (born Andrew Jakeman). They set the label up as a means of wanting to be able to push through the barriers of having to deal with the bureaucracy and reluctance of major labels when it came to giving new artists and new ideas a chance. The idea apparently occurred to Riviera whilst he was working as tour manager for Dr Feelgood on a US leg of a tour.

Riviera said in *Melody Maker* in August 1977; "I spent years shouting at people over desks in record company offices. They turned down virtually every idea I offered them. I decided I could do it without them. Kids are hipper and brighter than most record companies think. Stiff is interested in reaching those kids, right. I'm not interested in handing out stacks of free records and tee shirts and free lunches to journalists and dealers. I'm interested in the kids who buy the records, not the music business. And I want to offer those kids a good deal... we only sign people who've got a clear sense of direction, people who are bright. People who've got a grip on it."

It was Nick Lowe who first heard Costello's demo tape and it was on such basis that Costello was signed. (The two had met before when Costello was a fan of the Brinsley Schwarz band, in which Lowe played bass. Lowe told *Circus* in June 1978; "He even roadied for us for a while.").

By this point, Stiff had already signed Nick Lowe, as well as Ian Dury and The Blockheads. Lowe was on board not only as a musician, but as a producer and all-round admin person. Riviera was assigned to manage Costello and it was he who decided that the man born as Declan Patrick MacManus should move on from using the stage name of D.P. Costello to Elvis Costello. It was Lowe who helped Elvis to get his big break. He pointed him in the direction of Jake Riviera at the newly-formed Stiff Records. Lowe produced both *My Aim Is True* and *This Year's Model*.

Jake Riviera said in *Creem* in February 1978; "Elvis's tape was actually the very first tape we received at Stiff. It was so weird because I immediately put it on and thought, 'God, this is fuckin' good' — but at the same time I was hesitating because after all it was the first tape and I wanted to get a better perspective. So I phoned up Elvis and said, 'Listen, I've listened to your tape, it sounds really good and I'm interested, but could you give me a week in which to check out a bunch of other tapes and I'll get back to you?' Elvis said 'Fine' and so I waited a week, received a load of real dross in the mail and immediately got back in touch."

So what was on the demo tape? Costello told *Rolling Stone* in September 1982; "On the first demo tape that I sent to Stiff, that bought me the gig, as it were. There were only two or three songs that ended up on *My Aim Is True*. There were a lot of raw songs — and looking at them now — rather precious songs, with a lot of chords. Showing-off songs. I was very impressed by Randy Newman and wrote a lot of songs in that ragtime feel. I was very impressed with those funny chord changes that he used to play and I was emulating them on guitar. They came out convoluted; they weren't poppy at all, they had pretensions to a sophistication they didn't have. That exactly coincided with punk. But I was working — I didn't have the money to go down to the Roxy and see what these bands were doing: The Clash, the Pistols. I just read about them in *Melody Maker* and NME like everyone else. Joe Public. I was living in the suburbs of London; I couldn't afford to go to the clubs uptown. They were open until two o'clock in the morning, and I couldn't afford taxis — the tubes are all closed just after midnight. All these bands were playing in the middle of the night. I don't know who went to the bloody gigs — I can only guess they were rich people with cars and lots of drugs. I got up at seven in the morning and so I couldn't go. I was married with a son, so I couldn't take the day off. I took enough time playing sick, taking sick time off of any job, just to make *My Aim Is True*. Then I started listening to the records that were coming out, because I'd got this snobbish attitude: So little of any worth had come out for a few years. When the first few punk records came out, I suddenly started thinking: 'Hang on — this is something a little bit different'."

By October 1976, Costello was recording some solo demos at Pathway Studios in London. It was at this point that Riviera decided to team him up with a band who he had recently signed, Clover. At the time, Clover included John McFee (who later went on to be of Doobie Brothers fame) on pedal steel guitar and Huey Lewis. The latter didn't feature on *My Aim Is True* because his skills as a vocalist and harmonica player were surplus to requirements.

Pairing Costello with Clover — along with putting Nick Lowe as producer — resulted in *My Aim Is True* being recorded within just twenty-four hours of studio time over the period of December 1976 and January 1977. A lot of the material had been prepared prior to the studio time taking place.

Costello told *Rolling Stone* in September 1982; "I wrote a lot of songs in the Summer of 1977: 'Welcome To The Working Week', 'Red Shoes', 'Miracle Man', 'Alison', 'Sneaky Feelings', ' Waiting For The End Of The World', 'I'm Not Angry'. All more or less in one go, in about two or three weeks."

It was considered in *Circus* in February 1978; "*My Aim Is True* was recorded during his days off from work, with the assistance of

Elvis Costello - *This Year's Model*: In-depth

his producer Nick Lowe, who shared similar visions and ideas for instrumentation. It comes as little surprise when Elvis admits the record was cut with radio in mind." To which he was quoted, "I love the sound of the album because I love things that sound great on the radio. The record isn't for people with expensive stereos. I don't want my records to be used to demonstrate stereos, I just want people to listen to the music."

Prior to the release of *My Aim Is True*, Stiff issued 'Less Than Zero'/'Radio Sweetheart' as a single in March 1977. It didn't do well commercially and as a result, there were doubts as to whether an Elvis Costello album would be released at all. Fortunately, two more singles were released — 'Alison' and '(The Angels Wanna Wear My) Red Shoes'. The latter was met with positive critical acclaim but commercially it still floundered.

With things still looking uncertain, Costello agreed to quit his job as a computer operator at a cosmetics company when Riviera and Robinson agreed to match his wages which were, apparently quite humble. The BBC wouldn't play Costello's first single, 'Less Than Zero'. He was quoted on the matter in *Creem* in May 1978; "They didn't ban it. They just wouldn't play it. If it had been banned, at least I could have gotten some notoriety. 'God Save The Queen' wasn't banned because it attacked Her Majesty. It was because the Pistols went on the telly and swore. If there's one thing the English can't stand, it's bad language."

'Less Than Zero' was included on the LP, *A Bunch Of Stiffs*. It was released in April 1977 — a compilation designed to function as a sampler to get people interested in the artists signed under the label. Other artists included on the LP were Nick Lowe, Motörhead, Sean Tyla, Martin Stone, Dave Edmunds, Wreckless Eric and Magic Michael. Costello was quoted in *Rolling Stone* in September 1982; "We cut the first singles without any impact. My immediate reaction was, 'Well, maybe I haven't got it.' If I'd been somebody like John Cougar, signed to a major label — I suppose someone with a five albums for a million dollars deal — I suppose I would have felt, 'Well I'm secure now, I can write some songs,' but I wasn't sure. Stiff was running week to week — we were totally independent, we weren't licensed, we had no national distribution; it was mail-order. We finished the album in six-hour sessions; there were no days in the studio. Jake said, 'Well, we're going to put it out — but one moment it was going to be Wreckless Eric on one side, me on the other, as a way of presenting two or more writers. There were a million ideas floating around; it was all improvised and all governed by a very limited budget."

Whilst things were still looking tentative commercially, the important thing is that Costello still had the support of the Stiff label behind him and consequently, his music was starting to garner attention on the basis that it was so different. Structurally, it still adhered to verse/chorus and instrumentally, it was very typical of most rock bands but the content and the delivery in terms of Costello's lyrics and his vocals, well, it was those that stuck out.

Costello was compared to Bob Dylan by some. It was on the basis that his lyrics offered a social commentary in a way that was angry and yet highly musical, so much so that, like Dylan, his music portrayed a similar range and extent of emotions in a way that really spoke to some people. Articulate, intelligent lyrics communicated in a very stylised way. However, in response to being asked his thoughts on how he had been compared to Bob Dylan, Costello told *Melody Maker* in March 1978; "I don't give a shit. I've already forgotten who Bob Dylan was."

My Aim Is True was reviewed in *It's Only Rock 'N' Roll* in March 1978; "If not the album of the year then certainly the most exciting debut in an already important year for rock. Elvis Costello doesn't look like your average beautiful rock star. He's an ugly duckling with short, thatched hair and Buddy Holly glasses; the kid down the block whose mom made him study when the rest of the neighbourhood was playing. He could be you or me on this classic piece of rock 'n' roll vinyl. His musical influences are fifties and early sixties rock. His thin, nasal vocal style leans towards Graham Parker. Although more rock 'n' roll than Motown, with a dash of Nick Lowe with the old Brinsley Schwarz band. This LP is deftly produced by Lowe who also produced Parker. Originally released on Stiff records, CBS heard Costello and decided to see if he could reach a larger audience. Listening to Elvis Costello is like discovering rock 'n' roll for the first time! 'I won't get any older, now the angels wanna wear my red shoes,' he sings in 'Red Shoes', and the childlike imagery of never growing up is what rock is all about. 'Mystery Dance' is a brilliant

Elvis Costello - *This Year's Model*: In-depth

first experience with sex metaphor that has fifties classic written all over it. 'I'm Not Angry' has Elvis' romantic vulnerability combined with raw rage and a bitter guitar riff which displays the neurotic urgency that runs through the whole LP. Closely tied to 'Angry' is 'Alison', a bittersweet ballad about the duality of an old lover and the complex inner feelings of a man dealing with the problem. 'Less Than Zero', the British hit single, is about neo-Nazi Oswald Mosley having his own TV show on the BBC and a few other things that make 'everything seem less than zero.' All songs are beautiful linkups of melody and lyrics that you can dance to and listen to. Along with Lennon, Dylan, Davies, Townshend and Newman, Elvis Costello emerges as one of the most original and creative minds in rock 'n' roll. Buy this album and catch the 'Ratio Sweetheart' single on the *Hits Greatest Stiffs* import LP."

My Aim Is True was reviewed in the *Kingman Daily Miner* in March 1978; "In cuffed jeans and black square-rimmed glasses, Elvis Costello comes straight from the street with a simple message — Elvis Costello. The album's simple package — two pictures of the pigeon-toed Costello with his guitar (no lyrics or studio credits) — leaves us wondering whether or not he's for real. One spin of the disc dispels all doubts. *My Aim Is True* contains thirteen (count 'em!) tracks of simple, pure, and very authentic rock 'n' roll. The introverted Costello of the album cover becomes an extrovert in the studio. Costello's clenching high-tension vocals, backed by rhythm tracks direct from the high-energy and uncomplicated days of the sixties, make way for an unpretentious and highly contagious sound. And the final touch of truth is displayed in his lyrics, which range from an off-beat sense of humour ('Blame It On Cain') to an almost pathetic sensitivity to the trials and tribulations of love ('Alison' and 'Miracle Man'): Producer Nick Lowe, working for Keepitasahobby Productions, has captured the magic of Elvis Costello, who might be an ordinary rock 'n' roller out of his time zone, and this is just what puts *My Aim Is True* right on target!"

It was reviewed in the *Kingsport Times News* in January 1978; "Now I don't know, but I've been told that this guy is the next star of rock 'n' roll. Elvis sounds a lot like Bruce Springsteen (of rock 'n' roll past) and Graham Parker. He is interesting, to say the least. 'Welcome To The Working Week' sounds like an early sixties song, and 'Alison' sounds like a hit. Elvis looks weird and is musically bizarre at times, but he seems to have what it takes to make it — i.e., talent. And in these days of the New Wave, how sweet it is to see!"

Circus reviewed *My Aim Is True* in January 1978; "This not-wanting-to-be-famous stuff is provoking. It's easy for the British novelist Anthony Powell to sniff around the subject with amusement — novelists never have to come to terms with an audience as massive as that of a rock star. But Elvis Costello is another matter: *My Aim Is True* is an album of pungent rock and roll songs, and many of them sound like hits. This record has the richest, most intriguing set of lyrics of any since Neil Young's *Tonight's The Night*. Young deals with stardom by ignoring it, but Costello, already one of the greatest feisty rockers ever, wants to stand in the spotlight and beat the shit out of it. He works in the realm of sublime impossibility. To a person of Powell's generation (he is seventy-two), the sin of fame lies in its exposure of thoughts and actions that should — in a moral and socially correct sense — remain discreet. These are just the things that Costello, twenty-two years old, wants to toss in our face. No, the repulsion that this young Englishman feels for celebrity is for its privilege: All around him, he sees rock stars whose position does not oblige them to sustain the hard work that it took for them to become famous in the first place. Fame fosters laziness and dulls the creative rage on which great rock and roll feeds. These beliefs link Costello to English punk bands like the Sex Pistols and The Clash, but those groups do without Costello's fascinating stylistic contradiction of the nihilism that his lyrics proclaim — his echoes of people like Buddy Holly, Van Morrison, Johnny Rivers, and Bob Dylan. And so, naturally, Elvis Costello makes his own bid for first fame: because it will allow him to be heard by a large audience, because it grants him some power to get back at a lot of people who have wronged him. He doesn't want to be famous so that he can isolate himself — it's isolation that all of his songs rail against. Isolation, and a few other things. I said before that Elvis Costello seeks to expose private thoughts and actions. This isn't wholly accurate because it implies a kind of naughty daring that Costello might think beneath him. Where Johnny Rotten shrills with contempt at groupies (and groupies equal women for poor, wonderful Johnny), Elvis Costello is sorrowfully severe in, say, 'Alison'. His anger is specific, and he takes great pains to make clear, to us and to Alison, precisely what he resents — in this case, her blatant duplicity."

The review continued; "The punks frequently disseminate pure rage, to be used by the audience for its own purposes. For Costello, rage is far less potent and cathartic if it is that generalised; its ability to claim revenge is blunted when it is not specific. And so, although Costello is by no means a feminist sympathiser — like all hardcore romantics, he bases his world view on the old sexist system — he is startlingly decent. His values may be rigid, but they apply to everyone; cross him, be you woman or man, and you'll get cut. Eventually. *My Aim Is True* has a thin, sharp sound. Costello's voice and lead guitar sit on top of the mix. The background instruments are either confidently spare or furiously busy, and both styles are perfectly correct for their respective songs. The retarded drum thwak that begins 'Waiting For The End Of The World' sounds like it's coming from the inside of a sealed oil drum and it makes the stomach quiver in anticipation of Costello's menacing vocal. Elvis Costello's vocals do a lot more than menace — he can croon with lunatic abandon ('Alison', 'Sneaky Feelings') or yowl ('Miracle Man', 'I'm Not Angry') in a voice that is all bold nasality. Sometimes that voice seems to emanate from a sinus in his horn-rims. Costello's great accomplishment on this debut album is to blend bitter scepticism with romantic innocence. He is acutely aware of this paradox, arid, to protect its delicacy, he tries to bury the revealing awkwardness of personal history — on 'Pay It Back', he sings 'I wouldn't say I was raised on romance...' — even as he captures precisely that. 'Mystery Dance' is a nervous metaphor for a first sexual experience, 'Less Than Zero' posits an affable fatalism, and 'Miracle Man' decries a lover's unrealistic expectations. If the singer's subject matter leaps, his obsessions remain constant and thrilling in their unceasing intensity. In this, as in so much else on *My Aim Is True*, Elvis Costello is admirable. Better yet, he is heroic, in both the classical and vulgar senses. It's been a long time since I've had a hero. I've got one now."

My Aim Is True was reviewed in *Creem* in February 1978; "This bandit summer, this snatcher of heroes, loved ones and possibilities, will be remembered also for leaving behind intoxicating rock and roll, with this album near the top of the pile. Since August, competing for attention as a Stiff import with posthumous programming of

Why This Year's Model?

Costello's namesake's output, *My Aim Is True* has been an antidote to the power failure all around us. In his preoccupation with frustration and mental revenge, his cynicism stemming from a realisation that life's guarantees are worthless, and his imperturbably buoyancy in the face of it all, Elvis Costello is a contender. It doesn't even hurt that he styles himself a fifties schlemiel — his voice is captivatingly abrasive, his songs are, without exception, expertly crafted miniatures: there are thirteen here (Columbia added his new UK single), and not one your stylus begs to skip, not one that doesn't reveal something special about Costello's sensibility or talent. Every song has ideas to burn and a memorable chorus. The title (from the hauntingly tough-tender 'Alison') speaks chapters: his aim — his purpose and prowess — is true. Yes, you can call it "New Wave" — a tactical combination of the anarchic and the absorption of "classical" influences. *My Aim Is True* is so dramatic an entrance, such a total picture of its maker's worldview and personal use of rock grammar, that it's like *Breathless*. A B-movie with a difference. Even Costello's moral stance fits. He's a sensitive punkabilly, continually getting dumped on by girls. In his (our) world, the men are romantics, looking for touchstone love; the women more practical and self-preserving. Belmondo and Seberg. 'We could sit like lovers staring in each other's eyes...' he sings. On '(The Angels Wanna Wear My) Red Shoes' a strange Faustian bargain doesn't prevent a girl from telling him to drop dead as she leaves with someone else; on 'I'm Not Angry', another tale of rejection, the key word is 'anymore': one suspects that anger stopped only when turned into art. Girls are hard to please, he discovers on 'Miracle Man'; they make comparisons, and fools of men who leave their wounds open. Costello is so tormented by this treatment that he makes the inability to do the 'Mystery Dance' seem a sexual dysfunction."

The review continued; "And all the time this tension is going on — he does have other subjects, like ad hoc guilt transferral ('Blame It On Cain'), the horrors of employment ('Welcome To The Working Week') and surrealistic depictions of societal breakdown ('Waiting For The End Of The World', 'Watching The Detectives', 'Less Than Zero') — the music, the Nick Lowe-produced environment for all this rancour, is sensational. If he's his own lead guitarist (the wholly admirable musicians are anonymous), he's got the touch — economical, versatile, adept. Snappy rockers alternate with modern

Elvis Costello - *This Year's Model*: In-depth

blues, lovely ballads, mood pieces. 'Sneaky Feelings' crackles and pops. 'No Dancing' reminds us that a wall of sound is next to nothing without a gliding melody beneath. Throughout, there's witty background singing and spare, aggressive playing, close in spirit to The Rumour (as vocally Costello is temperamentally akin to Graham Parker). The only questionable aspect of Elvis Costello is how far he'll take his misogyny, how long he'll keep blaming women because he was raised on romance and has had it pulled out from under him. He snarls, 'Everybody loves you so much baby...' with the passion of mid-sixties Jagger, and it's great, it's even honest, and lesser men have made such sentiments springboards for whole careers. But such petulant putdowns indicate that he has some way to go before his emotional maturity matches his prodigious artistic skill."

Within the stable set up of a rock band, Costello's music was rhythmically vibrant and melodically sweet enough to carry some of the bitterness in the lyrics, almost as a remedy to them — but not quite. Guilt, bitterness and anger, Costello's lyrics embraced them all. They sat in line with the drama surrounding his image. He was quoted in *Creem* in February 1978; "The only two things that matter to me, the only motivation points for me writing all these songs are revenge and guilt. Those are the only emotions I know about, that I know I can feel. Love? I dunno what it means, really, and it doesn't exist in my songs."

With *My Aim Is True* already in the bag, The Attractions were grouped together upon Stiff's acknowledgement of the positive reception that Costello had received — particularly during a very early publicised live gig of his that took place at the Nashville Rooms in West Kensington, London on 27th May 1977. It was after this gig that Stiff placed an advert in *Melody Maker* in search of musicians to form a "rocking combo".

Admittedly, The Attractions were not a band of virtuosos. Their talent was arguably in the fact that they were precise, reliable and skilled within the framework of the music they made. On drums, there was Pete Thomas. He had previously played with Chilli Willi and The Red Hot Peppers. No relation to the latter, Bruce Thomas was on bass. He had played with Quiver and The Sutherland Brothers before coming out of retirement to play with Costello. Steve Nieve (born Stephen Nason, later named Steve Naïve and then Steve Nieve) was

Why This Year's Model?

recruited from the Royal College of Music to play keyboards. Steve must have been quite the character; it is said that during his audition he fell asleep while other keyboard players were trying to impress.

It was Riviera who decided to call the band The Attractions. Such was the working dynamic between Costello and The Attractions that it wasn't unusual for new songs to take shape over the course of live gigs. One such example is 'Hand In Hand'. When new songs weren't in the equation, the band played classics such as Abba's 'Knowing Me Knowing You', Ian Dury's 'Upminster Kid', Bacharach's 'I Don't Know What To Do With Myself', the Damned's 'Neat Neat Neat', Wreckless Eric's 'Whole Wide World' and Richard Hell's "Love Comes In Spurts'. Ultimately, a fun and varied repertoire.

Not long after they had formed, Elvis Costello and The Attractions played their first gigs just before the July 1977 release of *My Aim Is True*. Consequently the band that was making an impression with their live performances was not the same one that featured on Costello's debut. However, Costello's work was met with a positive reception; both in terms of *My Aim Is True* and the music that he was performing live with The Attractions.

My Aim Is True got into the UK top twenty and it wasn't long after that 'Watching The Detectives' was released as a single (it got to number fifteen. The song was produced by Nick Lowe with Steve Goulding on drums and Andrew Bodnar on bass. Organ overdubs were done by Steve Nieve).

July 1977 also saw Riviera encourage Costello to do a publicity stunt in the form of busking outside a hotel on London's Park Lane during a conference being held there by CBS with their US executives. Although it resulted in Costello being arrested for obstruction, the risk paid for itself when just days later, Costello was signed to CBS' Columbia Records in the US.

Costello was quoted in *Audio Scene Canada* in July 1978; "Ever since I had first started peddling my songs, some people at Columbia Records had shown a fair amount of interest in me. But they hadn't been able to convince the rest of the company — people who hadn't heard me — that I was a good investment. I realised that I would have to come up with a way of being heard by the rest of the company. As it happened, Columbia was holding its annual convention in London. So I went over to the hotel and busked outside the convention. I

Elvis Costello - *This Year's Model*: In-depth

had a little practice amplifier strapped to my shoulder and used my electric guitar. The timing was perfect because it was just when the convention was breaking for lunch, so I was heard by the president, the vice-presidents, and all the other important people at Columbia. They were impressed, as it turned out. Unfortunately, the Hilton Hotel where Columbia was holding the convention didn't see the joke, and the police were called. The police also failed to see the joke and I got arrested. I was released a few hours later. I wouldn't say that was the sole reason why I was signed to Columbia. But it did break the ice and allowed me to get through to the whole company in one day." Needs must. Costello was quoted in *Crawdaddy* in March 1978; "Columbia was one of the big companies who were the enemy at the time. They weren't paying attention."

Although the stunt was suggestive of a rebellion against the music industry and ultimately played a part in the making of Costello's public image, it ironically functioned as a vehicle to take him in a more commercial direction, especially in the US. It included a TV appearance on *Saturday Night Live* as well as the fact that although *This Year's Model* was ready for release, it was delayed for a little while in order that the label could get as many sales as possible from the re-release of his debut album.

Regarding how things had changed with their success, Nick Lowe was quoted in *Circus* in June 1978; "It's kind of fun, because just a few months ago people wouldn't have pissed on us if we were on fire; they thought we were losers, you know, but we just stuck at it."

Costello told *Creem* in February 1978; "When I played earlier in front of all those reps or whatever they're called — all those guys working for Island — did you hear me introducing 'Lip Service'? — 'This song is called 'Lip Service' and that's all you're gonna get from me.' That was straight from the heart, that, 'cos last year I actually went to Island with my demo tape and none of them wanted to know. Back then they wouldn't give me the time of day. But now..."

Intelligent production and effective management ensured Costello was promoted to a receptive audience. Playing live and loud in front of the London hotel where CBS held a convention was a risky move but it worked wonders with Elvis securing a US distribution deal with Columbia. Talent, good music and intensive touring did the rest.

Chapter Two

The Making Of This Year's Model

This Year's Model is reported to have had some quirky working titles; *Little Hitler*, *Girls! Girls! Girls!* and *The King Of Belgium*. The title of the album is actually derived from two of the songs that feature on the UK version of the album; 'This Year's Girl' and '(I Don't Want To Go To) Chelsea', which contains the lyric about "last year's model".

Not long after the single release of 'Watching The Detectives', work on *This Year's Model* began at London's Eden Studios towards the end of 1977. It was completed in early 1978. An impressive achievement considering that the studio time had been booked to fit into a small window of time in between touring. It was during these sessions — over approximately eleven days — that at least twelve songs were recorded, including, 'Pump It Up', '(I Don't Want To Go To) Chelsea', 'No Action', 'Lipstick Vogue' and 'Radio, Radio'.

Most of the songs that made an appearance on *This Year's Model* had already been part of the setlist since the band's live gigs in July 1977. 'Pump It Up', however, had been written during the last few days of the Live Stiffs package tour. In October 1977, Riviera had left Stiff Records, taking Costello and Nick Lowe with him. As a result, *This Year's Model* was Costello's first release on the Radar label. Riviera formed Radar Records with Andrew Lauder, former A&R director of Liberty/United Artists Records. Radar was distributed by WEA, who demanded exclusive UK distribution rights.

Costello's appearance on *Saturday Night Live* was a stroke of good fortune on the basis that the Sex Pistols were originally due to appear but they cancelled at the last minute. Even this early on in his career, Costello wasn't afraid to take risks; he gestured to The Attractions to cease playing just a few bars into 'Less Than Zero' and announced to the audience that the song was "not relevant" and instead, they were going to perform 'Radio, Radio'.

Such rebellious spontaneity was such that Costello was banned from the show (it wasn't until 1989 that he was invited back!). It was to Costello's advantage though in terms of how it generated a public image of notoriety — especially on the basis that a no interviews policy was adopted thereafter (it wasn't to last, but still). It's exciting to think that having made their mark on TV in such a stark way, Costello and The Attractions then returned to Eden Studios to finish off *This Year's Model*. It was during this time that *My Aim Is True* made it into the top forty in the US.

Even prior to its release, *This Year's Model* was a highly anticipated record. It was reported in *New Musical Express* in January 1978; "Ever since his Haitian divorce from the Stiff Records roster, ex-computer operator Elvis Costello has been keeping a deceptively low profile. Fans needn't worry though — our hero has been busy in the studios laying down a host of new meisterwerks for his imminent first Radar release. Tracks definitely for inclusion on this album will include 'The Beat', 'Lipstick Vogue', 'Lip Service', 'Pump It Up', 'No Action' and 'Little Triggers' — already tried-and-true faves from consistent live performance these last six months. Choosing the perfect single from this plethora of gems has been a real wrench for Messrs. Lauder, Riviera and Costello — though this dilemma has been finally resolved with the democratic choice of '(I Don't Want To Go To) Chelsea', which just tipped the scales over that other incendiary Costello evergreen, 'Radio, Radio'. Look for 'Chelsea' to appear soonest alongside Nick Lowe's first Radar single, 'I Love The Sound Of Breaking Glass' (wherein "powerpop" and Bowie's Lowe-styled cold music allusions are mated in truly extraordinary fashion). Fans of Mr Lowe will also be pleased to know that along with production credits on Elvis' up-and-comer, the irrepressible Basher's first solo album, entitled *Jesus Of Cool*, is all tied up and ready to be shipped. The finished cover slick is even now hanging grandly over Andrew Lauder's temporary Radar location in the United Artists complex. Costello, meanwhile, was due last Saturday — weather permitting — to fly out with his Attractions for a second stab at the Americas (where *My Aim Is True* has now gashed its way proudly into the halcyon realms of the top fifty album charts)."

The Making Of This Year's Model

The report continued; "The day before, fresh from that quirky *Today* interview on't telly where Mavis Nicholson's favourite rock star was quizzed blankly about the Sex Pistols break-up, Costello performed an impromptu free gig at the Roundhouse — more yer warm-up dress rehearsal job for the E.C. collective after those months ensconced in the studios than any kind of major gig. Even so, the gig was splendid, with Costello getting wilder than ever, tossing his guitar aside and confronting a rabid three hundred or so directly in front of the stage towards the end of the show. Starting with 'Radio, Radio' and spitfiring through a mixture of all the aforementioned new album sections plus *Aim* works like 'Waiting For The End Of The World' and 'Red Shoes', Elvis finished with a totally-deranged 'Detectives' and returned for one encore of 'Pump It Up'. A second encore was dramatically called off after Costello, having faced a torrent of gobbing throughout the set, found a specimen of said mucous in the glass he was drinking out of to quench his thirst on stage and stormed off in disgust. Still, all in all it was a magnificent set with special nods of approval to organist Steve Nieve, whose keyboard work was truly superb in the Garth Hudson epic-proficiency sweepstakes. With 'Chelsea', the new album and a British tour straight after those through to March US dates, world domination surely cannot be far away for Whitton's favourite son."

Early issues of *This Year's Model* came with a free 7" single. Housed in a Radar sleeve, the A-side featured 'Stranger In The House' which was an outtake from Costello's first album (it wasn't included on Costello's debut because sounding like a country song, it was considered to be too much of a commercial risk). On the B-side was a live cover of The Damned's 'Neat Neat Neat'. With Radar being a new label, they were clearly keen to think creatively when it came to promotion of both themselves and other artists.

And anyway, after setting up Stiff with Dave Robinson, having got so many strong artists on the label and a lot of general gravitas in the first place, why had Riviera chosen to leave and start something new? Costello was quoted in *19* in July 1978; "Basically, the Stiff personality was Jake, the main ideas came from him. Everyone does a grand job on the running of the actual thing but the basic personality of the label came from him. He decided he could do a better job on the two of us as personal manager than he could on the overall

Elvis Costello - *This Year's Model*: In-depth

label in question. He'd proved his point with Stiff. He started with nothing and got albums into the charts when everyone else thought those particular artists were a joke. In effect, we are all people that other labels regarded as a nuisance. I'd been written off by a number of labels. Ian Dury couldn't get signed, neither could Wreckless Eric. We had all been treated like jokes by most labels because they were afraid of anything that they didn't already have some idea of. If Phonogram had signed me up they would have given me a horn section and a couple of keyboard players and groomed me as the second Graham Parker because the minute I started playing they said I sounded like Graham Parker. Now I can't see that at all. The danger is that if you do happen to sound like someone, and you're almost bound to sound like someone, lots of labels don't have the imagination to exploit what's individual about you. They just exploit what is similar to someone else because they happen to know it sells. Having proved his point I think Jake decided it was time to jog on. He didn't want to get involved with Stiff Records in America. He realised that having gone that far, the rest would be boring. It would be just like empire-building. Atlantic Records started off exactly the same way as Stiff, from selling records off the back of a lorry into a multi-million-dollar corporation. I don't think they are having as much fun now as they had in the beginning. That was just pioneering the way Stiff was. Once the pioneering thing has gone, then it's boring."

'Radio, Radio' is a fascinating song because it documents something that was seemingly a very passionate subject matter for Costello. He had an insight into the music industry from an early age on the basis that his father, Ross MacManus, was a jazz trumpeter and cabaret singer. During his childhood, Costello had tagged along with him to a few live radio shows. In the early seventies, Ross MacManus was also responsible for the music and vocals for the *R. White's* Lemonade television advertisement theme song — 'Secret Lemonade Drinker' — on which his son sang backing vocals.

Ironically though, perhaps, by the time he had left school, Costello was working as a computer operator for a cosmetics company and living in a small flat in Acton with his wife and child. Around this time of his life, music featured in what must have been a frustrating capacity — in the form of rejections from record companies and playing a few small gigs on the side in the hope of something bigger and better. Annoyed at what he saw as tedious content on the radio at the time, Costello likened it to the rhythms of working at a computer. He was quoted in *Crawdaddy* in March 1978; "It was like a drone. The trains to and from work would play a part. Rhythms that go through your working day affect you, right? They had sort of a clattery sound — tk, tk, tk, tk — sometimes four o'clock in the morning is the only time you can get away."

'Radio, Radio' was apparently written in 1974, Costello was quoted retrospectively in *Far Out* in August 2020; "When I was sitting at home in England in 1975, in the thrall of Bruce Springsteen, he sort of made it feel like a big dream in America where a radio was playing and it was always the perfect song. And even though there's sadness in the song, I wanted to believe that somewhere it was like that and it wasn't like it was in the suburbs, where you couldn't hear any music you liked half the time. So that was a wishful song."

Overall, 'Radio, Radio' was anti-radio, with lyrics that picked a fight with the media and associated corruption and injustices that may or may not have been in place ("I wanna bite the hand that feeds me"). Costello said in *Audio Scene Canada* in July 1978; "In England, the BBC has a monopoly on what's played — and the playlists are very restricted. So I wrote 'Radio, Radio' as my reaction to the poor radio in England. But, when I got to America, I discovered that radio here is just as poor and the number of stations doesn't make it more interesting. There is a tremendous amount of good music available — music which none of the radio stations ever play."

Nick Lowe told *It's Only Rock 'N' Roll* in July 1978; "We almost didn't record 'Radio, Radio' because I thought it was a lousy song. A real dumper song with all that "anesthetise your mind" crap. And Elvis said, 'Okay, there's a million more where that came from.' Because he plays me tunes and he's so good that I don't feel any qualms about telling him if the bit doesn't cut it. But if he thinks it does he'll say 'You wait and see.' It's sort of a give and take thing. But we did it at a CBS convention in New Orleans and everyone was saying 'Great Nick. Can't wait to hear that 'Radio, Radio'!' And a couple of people nearly had heart failure when I told them we weren't recording it. So I thought I'd better do it. But we didn't put it out in England because it's too corny for there. But it's a really good record."

Elvis Costello - *This Year's Model*: In-depth

Costello spoke retrospectively in *Far Out* in August 2020; "You get into the business of making records and you realise what it's really about is some guy going off with a big sack of money to give it to somebody with hookers and cocaine so that they play your record enough times that people get batted to death with it and that makes it a hit."

The songs by other musicians that Costello performed live with The Attractions are suggestive that he had a broad range of musical influences. As much as he sometimes stated in interviews that there weren't any strong or specific influences, inspiration always comes from somewhere.

"I'm too young to remember rock 'n' roll, really," he said to *Crawdaddy* in March 1978. "I must have heard it, but I don't remember. The question of influence is pointless. I never list them except in a flippant way. There's no reason to assume that if I listen to Kenny and The Casuals, I'm going to go and write a song like them. I've had image-building work for and against me. The images get to be a burden because people expect them. I'm always interested in undermining whatever impressions people have of me. I went through all sorts of periods. For a while, I was writing nothing but country songs. I may still return to that. Problem is, some people think it's a joke."

When asked his opinion on New Wave bands, Costello said in *It's Only Rock 'N' Roll* in June 1978; "I take rock 'n' roll and musicianship seriously. I don't like groups who don't take it seriously and say, well, 'it's only rock 'n' roll'."

He told *Creem* in February 1978; "Gram Parsons had it all sussed. He didn't stick around — he made his best work and then he died. That's the way I want to do it. I'm never going to stick around long enough to churn out a load of mediocre crap like all those guys from the sixties. I'd rather kill myself. I mean, Parsons' exit was perfect... Well, not exactly like that I suppose. I see my exit as being something more like being run over by a bus. But, you think I'm joking, right — but I'm deadly serious about this. I'm not going to be around to witness my artistic decline."

The best clarification of how Costello regarded the idea of musical influences is plausibly from when he was quoted in *Audio Scene Canada* in July 1978; "I've never been obsessed with one person or band who I could say was a real influence on my form. Like everyone else, I hear all sorts of things that must have some sort of influence; but you never know how they'll come out again. For instance, I brought along a George Jones record for you to hear because I really like it — but I can't imagine that I'll ever start sounding like that. I like to think that my style is my own and I'm unique."

Years later, Costello was more candid about the music that he had grown up with. When speaking to *Rolling Stone* in September 1982 he said; "My father was with Joe Loss — the English Glenn Miller, I suppose. He was with him from about 1953 to 1968, and then he went solo; his instrument is trumpet but he's a singer. After the years with Joe Loss he went out as a cabaret artist; he does social clubs and nightclubs and cabaret, drives around himself. The first records I ever owned were 'Please Please Me' and 'The Folksinger' by John Leyton. I was at a bit of an advantage because my father was still with Joe Loss then — he used to get quite a lot of records because they would cover the hits of the day. He'd often have demonstration copies, even acetates; as late as 1966, Northern Songs would still send Beatles acetates out to orchestras to garner covers for (live) radio play. I've got them at home. As my father was the most versatile of the three Joe Loss Band singers, I was fortunate — he got the records and just passed them on to me. I was just into singles, whatever was on the radio — The Kinks, The Who, Motown. It was exciting. I was in the Beatles fan club when I was eleven; I used to buy the magazines. The one kind of music I didn't like was the rock'n'roll — as a distinct (classic) form. The girl next door loved The Shadows and Cliff Richard — I thought that was really old hat. Someone who lived across the road from my grandmother liked Buddy Holly — I thought that was terribly old-fashioned. I couldn't understand why anybody liked it. It never occurred to me that someone as *archaic* as Chuck Berry could have written 'Roll Over Beethoven' — because I was quite convinced George Harrison had written it. The only time it changed, the only time it went a bit peculiar, where maybe it went a bit *clandestine* was when I went to live in Liverpool. I was never very taken with psychedelic music — my dad went a bit psychedelic around the edges, about 1968. He grew his hair quite long; he used to give me Grateful Dead records,

Elvis Costello - *This Year's Model*: In-depth

and *Surrealistic Pillow*. I'd keep them for a couple of weeks and sell them at the record exchange and buy Marvin Gaye records. When I went to live in Liverpool I discovered everyone was into acid rock — and I used to hide my Otis Redding records when friends came around. I didn't want to be out of step. To the age of sixteen it's really crucial that you're in — and I tried hard to like the Grateful Dead or Spirit. I tried to find somebody of that sort that I could like that nobody else did — because everybody would adopt his group, and his group would be *it*; someone weird like Captain Beefheart. It's no different now — people trying to outdo each other in extremes. There are people who like X, and there are people who say X are wimps; they like Black Flag. I actually "saw the light" when I was already playing — coming back to London, seeing a lot of groups, Nick Lowe and the Brinsleys, pub-rock groups. I think you get very earnest when you're about sixteen to eighteen, and everyone at school was listening to either the psychedelic groups or the singer/songwriters; it was all very earnest, *pouring out your inner soul*. In London I discovered that all music that I liked secretly, that I'd been hiding from my friends — that was what was great fun in a bar: Lee Dorsey songs! Suddenly it was all right to like it; that was when I saw the light. There was nothing wrong with it... It was difficult to develop an original style. I have no idea who it was that I might have been imitating, whether consciously or unconsciously. I was playing on my own, trying to put my songs across. I suppose I should have had a band behind them — but playing alone did build up an *edge*. I did the odd show just to keep up, to keep trying to improve the ability to play. You'd soon know if a song was bad if you were dying in a club; you'd have to put more edge on it. Playing on your own, you'd have the tension — you could increase the tension at will, not relying on anyone else to pick up the beat."

As an English artist who was big in America, as with the Beatles, the content on Costello's albums was varied to accommodate his different audiences. He was quoted in the *Bastrop County Times* in July 1978; "The story behind that is basically that there's always one less track on an American album by an English artist. Album-programming is designed for groups like Santana who record three tracks on a side, and pad it out with lots of guitar solos. They're not really designed for people writing songs, and therefore record companies only pay for eleven tracks. They won't pay for any more, so an artist is giving the company tracks if he delivers more than eleven songs. I object to the idea of not being paid for the work, 'cause it's a professional job."

As well as there being one less song on the US version of *This Year's Model*, 'Radio, Radio' replaced '(I Don't Want To Go To) Chelsea'. The decision was made by Columbia. Costello was quoted in the same feature; "They wanted 'Radio, Radio' on the American album, and decided 'Chelsea' was rather English-oriented. We left it to them. And they kept the basic running order of the album... By the same token, 'Radio, Radio' is not on the English album, so there's talk at the moment of making it a single in England. 'Chelsea' could become an American B-side. It all depends. We might pioneer the return of the EP!"

The opening track, 'No Action', is full of manic excitement; it completely embodies the spirit of *This Year's Model*. Costello's lyrics are full of wordplay and imagery and in combination with the pulsing backing from The Attractions, it gives an explicit insight into what is to come. Costello was quoted in *Crawdaddy* in March 1978; "My album has no love songs. Not in the sense that I choose them. Quite a few of my reviews have tended to picture me as an emotional masochist. Well, many of the songs are involved with revenge and guilt. Some are about being tricked. These are the stronger feelings, the ones you are left with at night. Each song is how I felt when it was written, the spur of the moment."

Although slower, 'This Year's Girl' and 'The Beat' still contain an extent of aggression that is certainly attention-grabbing. In 'The Beat', the combination of a gravelly-sounding guitar with a rock 'n' roll melody is juxtaposed with lots of syncopated beats, so much so that even with the organ at the helm, the reggae influence comes through explicitly. 'Pump It Up' is bouncy and full of a rhythm that is perfect for pogo dancing. As a live number, it easily invited an intense response for the crowd. Costello was quoted in *Crawdaddy* in March 1978; "I'm more interested in people dancing than thinking, I don't like concepts. Individual things are more important. Being stood up on a date hurts more than a Big Concept."

In the liner notes for the 2002 reissue of *This Year's Model*, Costello stated that The Rolling Stones' *Aftermath* was an influence.

Elvis Costello - *This Year's Model*: In-depth

This particularly shines through on 'This Year's Girl'. The latter was reviewed in *Cash Box* in June 1978; "Elvis is thought by many to be one of the most important new artists to emerge during the last year. The first single from *This Year's Model* (produced by Nick Lowe) is a clever and meaningful statement about the double-edged adoration of idols. Tough, excellent singing, old-time organ and jaunty beat mesh effectively. Top forty pick." In response to the fact that one critic had called him a misogynist for 'This Year's Girl', Costello was quoted in *New Musical Express* in March 1978; "(It) is ridiculous because 'This Year's Girl', if anything, is like a female 'Miracle Man' in that they both deal with inadequacy — with humour, I believe. Like, 'This Year's Girl' is not one girl — it's a song for and about all the girls who desperately follow this year's trends; the Biba girls or Fiorucci or whatever. And I'm not castigating them personally for swallowing that myth. In fact it's almost compassionate in a way. If it's an attack, it's an attack on the idea, or the notion."

Costello said in *Rock Around The World* in February 1978; "I never said I was injecting anything moral into my music. I just do the thing the way I feel I should do it. I know the weaknesses in my music and that's what I have to live with. All the time I'm fighting a battle against myself to escape mediocrity and to do better. All creative people are like that. But the difference between myself and the vast majority of songwriters is that I'm not content with a sloppy phrase when a better one will do. How many people can honestly say that?"

Regarding 'Little Triggers', Costello told *New Musical Express* in March 1978; "It is a very weird song, yeah. Different things come to mind when I hear it now. It's more "evocative" than direct. More like a poem though I hate poetry usually. It's weird — the way I see it now, it relates very much to 'Alison'. It's like the reverse side of the feeling in 'Alison' though I certainly didn't plan it that way. Well that song is very, very personal to me and I rarely perform it now. Very rarely. I'm usually just not in the right mood. And it's almost frightening that, because when I find that feeling creeping up on me — when I perform that song — that I'm attaching more importance to my work than is reasonable. It's like 'yeah, it's only rock 'n' roll' but, at the same time, rock 'n' roll as such is my life. It's all I do, so these songs are me. That's why people whose songs you admire are usually so disappointing when you meet them. Because their songs are their lives and they don't have a life outside their songs. And often I feel exactly the same way."

What The Attractions contributed to *This Year's Model* is not to be underestimated. '(I Don't Want To Go To) Chelsea' originally made use of a guitar figure that was pretty much on the beat — very much in the vein of hard rock. With Bruce Thomas and Pete Thomas on board, a more syncopated rhythm was embraced. Steve Nieve used a Vox Continental organ with a cheap keyboard called an Instapiano. It had minimal sustain and volume until put through an amp.

In the liner notes of the 1989 album, *Girls Girls Girls*, Costello revealed that he took inspiration from The Who, The Kinks and The Clash, as well as The Pioneers for the writing of '(I Don't Want To Go To) Chelsea'.

It was asserted in *Melody Maker* in May 1978; "All that really needs to be said presently about *This Year's Model* is that it presents more than adequate evidence of Costello's remarkable maturity as a songwriter and performer, and a collective performance by his musicians that sets them at the vanguard of modern rock 'n' roll... Every song is marked by an inspiration that is all too rare at the moment... As far as I'm concerned, it's one of the definitive albums of this decade."

Overall, it is considered by many that The Attractions resulted in *This Year's Model* having a much fuller sound than that on *My Aim Is True*. Rhythmic ideas were expanded whilst the organ and guitars add swirling melodies in contrast to the harsh (but concise) drumming. The Attractions added to what Costello was doing rather than drawing attention away from it.

Overall, Costello and The Attractions offered a sound that was smart and ergonomic and yet certainly, not without strong musicality. Both '(I Don't Want To Go To) Chelsea' and 'Pump It Up' are consistently driven by their grooves, and whilst they embody the power and aggression that sits right up there with a lot of other punk and New Wave music that was happening at the time, there is a lot of lyrical and melodic originality in place.

'(I Don't Want To Go To) Chelsea' was released as a single in the UK on 3rd March 1978 with 'You Belong To Me' on the B-side. 'Pump It Up' followed on 28th April with 'Big Tears' on the B-side.

'(I Don't Want To Go To) Chelsea' was reviewed in *Sounds*

Elvis Costello - *This Year's Model*: In-depth

in March 1978; "Ol' four eyes is back. 'Chelsea', already well-known through concert and TV appearances, is in a similar style to 'Watching The Detectives' with the thundering reggae-like bass line, Costello's staccato guitar and the enduring sixties plastic organ sound. Memories of the Small Faces, 'Whatcha Gonna Do 'Bout It' and the Stones' 'Last Time' are stirred by 'You Belong To Me'. Not only does Chelsea justify the respect for Elvis, but caps a thrilling month with Nick Lowe and James Williamson welcoming Radar into the world."

In the same month, *New Musical Express* named '(I Don't Want To Go To) Chelsea' as the single of the week, reviewing it as follows: "The whole business is beginning to make me feel faintly sick. I mean, how Elvis Costello can just sit around making an apparently endless supply of records that are plainly and simply better than everybody else's except the Ramones and Muddy Waters is just beyond me. This single's so good that the very act of releasing it amounts to bragging on a colossal scale. Cases: a dark, chunky rhythm track, Steve Nieve's by-now-patented Garth Hudson lifts (check out Dylan's live version of 'All Along The Watchtower' from the *Flood* double), spiky, angry guitar interpolations from The Man Costello, a mordant insinuating vocal and the Nick Lowe production to end all Nick Lowe productions (fat chance). The song is a veritable blinder: a nightmare vision of the Swinging London of the mid sixties — and, by extension, now — with imagery drawn from *Blow Up* and *Smashing Time*. The line 'Call her Natasha but she looks like Elsie' is a direct reference to that latter movie, a hideous exploitation flick starring Lynn Redgrave, Rita Tushingham and Michael York. Put it this way: Nick Kent bet anyone in the office a fiver that 'Chelsea' would make top five and no-one would take him up on it. If Radar can maintain the standards set by their releases thus far, they should reign as unchallenged in their field as Costello does in his."

It was reported in *Melody Maker* in March 1978; "'You Belong To Me', the flip side of Elvis' new fab 45, '(I Don't Want To Go To) Chelsea', was written originally — we're sure you'll be simply enthralled to learn — for the Feelgoods. It was commissioned by Nick Lowe who produced the F Goods' *Be Seeing You* album. Basher thought, apparently, that the Feelgoods' repertoire could be brightened up by the inclusion of some new songs from the pens of hotshot new rock 'n' roll writers. Elvis, Graham Parker and Will Birch were all approached. Elvis' effort at least got as far as the recording studio before it was abandoned. The Feelgoods had no actual criticism of the song; they'd be the first to agree that it's an ace choon. It was simply that, like a lot of El's songs, it was rather, ahem, wordy. Too wordy for Lee Brilleaux, at least. It was only at the insistence of Lowe that Lee persevered with the song: 'Awright Bash, one more time,' he'd say wearily as he attempted once more to master the lyrics. Lowe remembers him standing in the studio at the microphone, scanning the endless verses on the lyric sheet and finally tossing it aside with an exasperated 'Ere, Bash, let's ditch this song — it's a bit War 'n' Piece (sic), innit?'"

Totalling just thirty-six minutes, *This Year's Model* is a relatively short album by today's standards, but that is arguably not to its detriment. It is short, sharp and to the point, just like the ascorbic lyrics that are painted across each song.

Costello told *Crawdaddy* in March 1978; "I write singles-length songs. If you can't get it down in three minutes, you ought to give it up. It's not mock anger that I express."

It is endearing how Costello seemed to advocate for simplicity in favour of overstating music as art. He said in *Creem* in May 1978; "That's the biggest problem with the last fifteen years of rock. People always claim it's art — and it's not. Don't get so esoteric. That's the problem with you critics — you try to make everything so complicated when it's not."

He was quoted in the *Bastrop County Times* in July 1978; "I don't claim to have any unique taste or any particular insight into music."

And in *Rock Around The World* in February 1978; "I'm only interested in songs. I don't know music and I don't write music as such. The only reason I care about music at all is that it is the only available medium for writing songs. But, at the same time, I don't consider myself a poet. I'm not obsessed with the written word. But it is the combination of the two that forms itself into a song which is the form I'm totally involved with."

Happy to leave the mixing to the producer, Costello explained to the *Bastrop County Times* in July 1978; "Nick concentrates on making it sound pretty loud. We don't go, like, instrument by instrument. We always like to play as a band. Sometimes we'll re-do the vocals and overset harmonies and extra instruments, but I always try to go for a basic four-piece sound to begin with."

In terms of how he preferred to produce songs, Lowe said in *Crawdaddy* in July 1978; "It doesn't matter if it's fifteen minutes long, if you make it with that singles mentality — Trim off all the spare, all the waffle, all the stuff you don't need. I don't like fiddlin' around with getting the sound organised too much, because you can do all that in the mix. Nowadays, with the gadgets they've got in studios, you can make anything sound like anything by twiddling a few knobs. I'm more interested in making sure the people who are recording are in a good frame of mind to perform right. All the rehearsal in the world can't get that enthusiasm, to get people ready to burn. You've got to be a bit of a psychologist. Some people, like Brinsley (Schwarz) — he only plays really good guitar when he's pissed off. So if I'm going to do an overdub later on, I'll needle him for an hour, so he's a bit pissed off at me."

This Year's Model has a very "live" feel to it and this is no coincidence. Nick Lowe said in *It's Only Rock 'N' Roll* in July 1978; "My philosophy to recording is to bash it down and then tart it up later in the mix. I don't make records for musicians or people in the music business. Because I've found out that the people who buy my records or albums by people I produce haven't got big expensive stereos. So I make records that sound dynamite on shitty stereos at very low volume. It's my specialty. What I try to do is make records which you don't have to be a musician to understand. And this entails capturing something on record that all the rehearsal in the world can't guarantee that you'll get. Something very spontaneous and special and I don't think you get that by spending three days trying to get a snare-drum sound. So what I do is set up the mics and get, as near as possible, the people to sing at the same time. Elvis is especially good at this because they just set up and sit round and he sings into the mic. The record comes out with all the solos and everything on it as opposed to overdubbing. The more you overdub the more sterile it gets and it's nothing you can put your finger on. You can't say, 'this record sounds sterile because.' I think there's a psychological element involved, one of believability. It's something that you can't plan. The best records that I've ever had anything to do with have all had that. You can only get that by three takes. If I can't get it in three takes I'll move on to something else."

Whilst Clover had been an asset on *My Aim Is True*, The Attractions sounded very in sync with Costello on *This Year's Model*. It was considered in *New Musical Express* in March 1978; "The Attractions are a band of sufficient calibre to allow Costello to do whatever he wants to do — or to hold down the song when Costello's guitar packs up on him, which it's been doing with alarming frequency during the preceding few dates — and still stay on the case. There's Pete Thomas on the drums, formerly of Chilli Willi and The Red Hot Peppers, John Stewart and The Wilko Johnson Band (though that's a dark little episode indeed), the epitome of clean-cut whompin', stompin', powerdrive. Bruce Thomas — formerly of The Sutherland Brothers and Quiver — plays bass in a manner that enables him to oscillate between the rhythm section and the front line or even occupy both territories simultaneously. He plays a lot like Rick Kemp, with whom he used to compete for sessions and whose salmon-pink Fender Precision bass he plays. On keyboards is Steve Nieve, a twenty-year-old drop-out from the Royal College of Music and all-purpose mutant. He can pick up and learn any style, riff or lick virtually overnight and lose any solid object known to mankind with equal alacrity. He has lost more cigarette lighters on this tour than most people own in a lifetime, and according to tour scuttlebutt he's been knocking down enough pussy these last six weeks to make Warren Beatty or Phil Lynott feel inadequate. The surreal washes, robotic bleeps and outrageous quotes that he inserts into the music complement Costello's idiosyncratic singing and guitar and the rhythm section's two-fisted power and tigerish agility with almost alarming appropriateness. What I'm saying is that Mr Costello has himself one screaming lulu of a band, an aggregation worthy of what he puts in front of it; one capable of outpunching most of the competition on their own turf and then moving with almost ludicrous ease into territories where lesser bands would never dare to tread."

It comes across that perhaps Costello regarded *This Year's Model* as a step up from *My Aim Is True*, at least in terms of its cohesiveness as an album. In *New Musical Express* in March 1978 he said; "I see the *Aim* songs as just "a collection", really. On *Model*, in the beginning, I was into creating something more complete —

Elvis Costello - *This Year's Model*: In-depth

not a concept album but something more interlinked, yeah? Back then there was still 'Detectives' which, actually though it's not on this album, 'Detectives' was very important because it was the first song that proved to me that I could write in a whole new style. Like, I see this album as being generally more "oblique" lyrically than *Aim*... Like, the imagery is generally far more fragmented, in songs like 'Chelsea' and 'Lipstick' — very much in a non-linear fashion. Like 'Chelsea' is more like snapshots intercut between two movies — *Smashing Time* and *Blow-Up*. But 'Detectives', which I wrote in the first twenty-four hours of constantly listening to the first Clash album which I'd just bought, was the first song where I discovered I could write in that fragmented style. But then again y'know, 'This Year's Girl' is very specific. It was so specific at first that it read like a chronicle. I didn't see any emotion in it until later on."

Regarding 'Living In Paradise', Costello said; "Actually it's a completely different version of a very old song from the *Aim* sessions with a really ancient last verse attached to it. That's the form anyway but no, it's actually me envisaging the future if I let certain things happen to me. This I do in two songs, one of which is 'Hand In Hand', the other being 'Paradise'. 'Paradise' itself is a notion, an idea of what people think would be paradise but which in effect is so totally decadent that, were they to go along with it, they'd end up just utterly corrupt and perverted. 'Hand In Hand' is more complicated. Like it stems — I wrote it in fact specifically for Nick Lowe, who rejected it because at the time he was more into two-chord things but, well, that doesn't matter so much as the fact that at the time of *Aim*'s mixing sessions, Nick was going through this incredible period of misery and depression as a result of the whole Rockpile episode with Swan Song and all that. Now I don't know Nick that well, though we work well together, but I don't socialise with him and I haven't seen his darker side, for example. But he was so obviously just totally "cut up" by this experience that I wrote 'Hand In Hand' as a consequence of it all not simply for him but also because the main figure — the Jimmy Page-type who is actually stating those things, and let's not beat around the bush here with Swan Song and all that crap — is just the sort of unhuman monster type I could become if I let myself go that far. So the song is totally given over to stating someone else's feelings with just the slightest tinge of, not "fear" but, yeah, that could just about be me, y'know. That's actually a proven example of what I meant when I spoke earlier about using other people as mouthpieces. It may one day totally get like that ... when I'm writing totally impersonal songs. See, I just can't carry on doing "more revenge". It'd be like The Clash singing 'White Riot '78' or something."

In his 2015 autobiography, Costello revealed that 'American Girl' by Tom Petty and The Heartbreakers formed the inspiration for 'Lipstick Vogue' (of course, the latter is certainly more high energy than the former, but still).

'Night Rally' concludes *This Year's Model*; a relaxed but appropriate way to wrap up what is predominantly a very upbeat album. Regarding some of the themes in *This Year's Model*, Costello said in *New Musical Express* in March 1978; "Well yeah, there is a quotient of vindictiveness there, but there are so many other things going on at the same time. For one, there are more positive aspects to, say, 'Lipstick Vogue' than are noticed. The chorus is, after all, 'you're not another mouth lost in the lipstick vogue.' That's positive. In fact the negative side is actually turned in on myself when I say 'Sometimes I almost feel/Just like a human being.' Because often I don't feel quite human — I don't feel real. And that song was written long before other people started describing me as "robotic" or "an android" and all that. It's almost like a self-fulfilling prophecy. In fact, there are quite a few things on this album that are like that. Frighteningly so, in fact. Things I've had absolutely no control over, at least four of the *Model* songs came true after I wrote them... First of all you could almost break down my two albums and put songs under headings. Like the first album, it was politics/philosophy (general)/ and revenge. And with *Model* you kinda go — politics, then fashion and then whatever else, there's some other heading in there too. See, 'Chelsea', 'Lipstick', 'Paradise', 'This Year's Girl', 'Pump It Up' are all kind of songs about "fashion" so they do relate to me now even though they were written before I became a "fashion". See, the self-fulfilled prophecy thing is exactly that: in a perverse way, I am currently becoming fashionable, a fashion unto myself. I never ever wanted that, mind you. It's very frightening in a way because that's the very last thing I ever wanted to become. From the very beginning there was never any air-brush stuff. I could never imagine a lot of people wanting this ugly geek in glasses ramming his songs down their throats. And that's exactly what I'm in it for. I'm in it to disrupt people's lives."

It seems that the working dynamic in the studio was professional and constructive; not necessarily something that was the product of a group of mates having a good time at the expense of the record label. Nick Lowe told *New Musical Express* in March 1978; "I don't mean that we're all loony chums perpetually having a great laugh together, any kind of let's-all-piss-it-up-chaps sixth form outing. I'm deadly serious about the whole thing. Vicious, even. I could be vicious about it. It's not like we're all part of the same chums club. That's why I like Elvis so much. He's deadly serious. He means it, maaaaaaan. It's not a drinking club. Bullshit. I mean, Jake (Riviera) and I have always had this agreement from the very start. It's like an agreement never to get too close because even though we like each other we respect each other for what we both do — and Elvis as well — and there's this element of keeping each other at a pole's length. All three of us are very committed in a very obscure way and if you're committed to something, you can never afford to cling onto something too tight, because it's a golden egg or he's a marvellous chum that you always want to be with. Because you can change your mind about people all the time. We've never actually talked about this: it's just how I feel. And it's this that keeps us tight, in a way. Okay, we're good buddies and everything, but always reserve the right to change your mind. You can go back on anything and not feel embarrassed or ashamed about it. You say, 'That was then; I've changed my mind. I'm really sorry, but I can't help it.' It's just an instinct that we all have. A recognition."

Full of tracks that make a point in a way that is succinct and memorable, *This Year's Model* signified the start of further success for Elvis Costello and The Attractions.

Chapter Three

Touring

As soon as Elvis Costello and The Attractions had finished recording the last few tracks for *This Year's Model*, they were off to America. Between January and March 1978, they played across nineteen states and finished with two nights in Toronto, Canada. They were recorded by Columbia and put on the promotional album, *Live At The Mocambo*. The following five weeks were dedicated to touring halls across England, Scotland and Ireland. With the last UK show being at the Roundhouse in London on 16th April, three days later saw the band begin another six weeks worth of US theatre dates, with which Nick Lowe and Mink DeVille supported. After this, Costello and The Attractions did their first tour of Europe prior to going to Eden Studios to record *Armed Forces*.

Costello was clearly quite the character to tour with. It was reported in *Crawdaddy* on March 1978 that "on the road, he carries an accountant's ledger which says "records" on the front cover and he scribbles constantly."

As fascinating as it would be to know what he was writing, we'll probably never know. Costello was probably a man in charge of his own game when touring in 1978. He was quoted in *Melody Maker* in the March of that year; "Just because someone gives me a good review doesn't mean that I'm going to fall at their feet. I don't need you (points to journalist), or you, or him, or anyone to tell me that I'm good. I know how good I am. I didn't need anyone to tell me that *This Year's Model* was a good album, I knew it was. I don't think it's the greatest album ever recorded. It's not going to stop the world. But I had the imagination to come up with that album, and I expect more imagination from the critics who wrote about it."

In response to the journalist's statement of "I've noticed others

Elvis Costello - *This Year's Model*: In-depth

saying about you — a strong body of opinion, so to speak, which was typified by something Ian Dury said about you in NME. It was something like — 'Oh yeah Elvis is a good songwriter but he's not a mature human.' — 'He is just a boy' I think was the exact reference,"

"Ah yes, a couple of people have said that. Nick (Lowe) said something similar and some people on the Stiff tour did as well. It usually takes the form of, yeah they think I'm a good songwriter — they've got a certain amount of respect for my songs — they think my talents are mature but they don't think I'm a mature human being. That I'm incomplete somehow as a human being. But then again, I'd agree with them. I'm not a balanced, mature person as far as I'm concerned. I don't want to sound like some weirdo, but still, they're right, yeah. I would back them up certainly."

In response to the *New Musical Express* question of, "Do you want to get more mature as a person and consequently get less extreme? Or do you consider those extremities, albeit immature or overly neurotic, as still indispensable as basic fuel for your songwriting?" Costello replied; "That's a difficult one. It's my 'Will he have difficulty relating to success and will he still be as sharp as he was now he's been pulled off the streets?' dilemma. That tends to be the popular one that people get with their second albums. It was like that for Springsteen, wasn't it? Like, 'What's he going to do now he's no longer on the streets in New Jersey?'... with me it's going to be 'What's going to happen now he's a success? How are the changes going to affect him?' Okay, well there are two ways around that. I could find myself "praying" with people, projecting myself through them in order to write songs. Which I've already done, by the way. And then there's a dimension beyond that where that thing becomes a dimension within itself. One new song of mine for example — 'Dr Luther's Assistant' — is a case in point. It's a new interest of mine — people owning people, people playing with other people like pawns. Not like a "pawn of society" or even a "pawn of the corporation". Just one-to-one. So that's one new thing that's still just as emotional as before. The other thing, you see, I don't necessarily think I'm going to become a "nicer person" or a more "complete" person as a consequence of all this. Because this job is not designed to make you nicer, or more mature even. You can say

— 'Oh you're just immature, you'll soften up' but I fuckin' won't because, say, tenderness. I can feel tenderness and I'm not afraid of it and it isn't entirely absent from either of my albums. It's just that everybody with their typical lack of imagination chose to ignore any signs of that completely and plump for the other extremities instead. See, people don't realise that I may not be mature because I may just not fuckin' want to be. I don't know what being grown-up is, see. And I don't think it's necessarily any better. In other ways though, sometimes I feel one hundred years old or certainly much older than I actually am. A lot of the time I think my reactions to many given situations are those of a middle-aged person — I'm not saying that's unique or anything — but therefore I do actively resent being called a "kid" because I know there's no set pattern of maturity. Christ, when I was eighteen — five years ago — I felt thirty and it's only in the last, say, three years that I've actually felt younger so to speak. At eighteen I was really deadly, deadly cynical, and it's only been in the last six months that I've been feeling much younger, much less serious. If only because I'm starting to see the whole joke — the great joke of life itself."

It is plausible that such approach informed how Costello performed on stage. Good. It was fierce and unapologetic in a way that often got the crowds fired up.

Was there an element of playing up to an image in the music press? Quite possibly. Having told the interviewer that he didn't consider himself as an artist or as a songwriter, Costello said; "My ultimate vocation in life is to be an "irritant"! Not something actively destructive just someone who irritates, who disorientates. Someone who disrupts the daily drag of life just enough to leave the victim thinking there's maybe more to it all than the mere hum-drum quality of existence."

A few years later, Costello offered a little more insight into things. In response to the interviewer's statement of "In your first interview, in 1977 with Nick Kent of NME, you made a famous statement: words to the effect that all you knew of human emotions were revenge and guilt. Those words have been endlessly quoted — I've quoted them, they're irresistible. Now you're describing that as venom — as if your artistic venom, what you put into your music,

Elvis Costello - *This Year's Model*: In-depth

had engulfed your own life," Costello told *Rolling Stone* in September 1982; "I think it did. I think it started to take over. You see, I think that after a while — apart from everything else, looking from a purely artistic point of view — it started to become a problem for me to incorporate the wider, more compassionate point of view that I felt; I was trying to put that forward in some of the songs, and it was so much at odds with the preconception of the image. When we were playing, the frustration of that just ate me up. And with the lack of personal control in my life, and my supposed emotions, and drinking too much, and being on the road too much — I'm not saying I wasn't responsible for my actions; that sounds like I'm trying to excuse myself. But I was not very responsible. There's a distinct difference. I was completely irresponsible, in fact. And far from carefree — careless with everything. With everything that I really care about. And I think that in as much as it was said that we fed ourselves to the lions, you could say that whatever the incident was, it was symptomatic of the condition I was in, and that I deserved what happened regardless of the intentions of the remarks."

Speaking to *Audio Scene Canada* in July 1978 Costello said; "I think it's the job of the record company to create demand for the artist's product and sell a lot of records. Certainly, I wanted to have hit records. I've never been interested in waiting around until my time for success comes. Above all, I've never subscribed to the theory that one should do the decent thing and endure a certain period of failure before having a hit record. I waited long enough to get the chance to make a record. For more than eight years, I practiced and wrote songs. Lots of bands don't succeed because they record before they're ready. But I was in a position where I had songs to choose from; I certainly wasn't restricted to the thirteen songs that are on the first album. Yes, I'm in business to sell records. And I expect the record company to spread the word. Quite a lot of the people who haven't bought my records probably haven't even heard of me, so it's not a question of whether they like my work. The record company is extremely important to the final outcome. I have some friends who are on the Secret Agent label — it's a very well-kept secret when their records come out." (The journalist noted that Costello seemed pleased to have the opportunity to show some humour in contrast to

Touring

his angry image).

Prior to the release of *This Year's Model*, great efforts had been taken to generate excitement in America. Not just regarding Costello, but of all the artists who had recorded on the Stiff label. Consequently, this may have added weight to the enthusiasm with which Costello and The Attractions were met with when they toured America.

For instance, Stiff Records ran a large scale promotional campaign to bring several UK artists to the attention of a US audience. As the banner in their newspaper advert put it, "America Gets Stiff." *Billboard* reported on this in February 1978; "Dutch record company Dureco is launching a big campaign on behalf of UK New Wave label Stiff under the banner "Great Stuff On Stiff," also the title of a live album featuring Elvis Costello, Nick Lowe, Ian Dury, Wreckless Eric and Dave Edmunds. The album was recorded at the London Lyceum in October last year when the show was also filmed for a fifty minute documentary which will be transmitted here. Dury gives his first Dutch concerts March 3-5 and his appearance at the Amsterdam Paradiso will be taped by VPRO Radio. Release of Wreckless Eric's debut album is lined up for the second week of March, the first 2,000 copies pressed on brown vinyl. During the campaign Elvis Costello's debut album *My Aim Is True* will be re-released, as well as the two Damned albums *Damned Damned Damned* and *Music For Pleasure* and the sampler LPs *Hits Greatest Stiffs* and *A Bunch Of Stiff*."

Costello was quoted in *New Musical Express* in March 1978; "Well of course, Americans have never produced one decent home-grown rock and roll band, so when they're confronted with the real thing they tend to get a little over excited."

Even before the release of *This Year's Model*, America had been given an insight into what they could expect. In March 1978, *Crawdaddy* reported on Costello's concert that took place on 7th December 1977 at The Hot Club in Philadelphia; "Ten o'clock now. The Hot Club is packed shoulder to shoulder; it's impossible to get to the bar. The line for the late show stretches down the icy block outside. Costello is pushing full-throttle towards the climax of his set. He is lobster red; the veins in his neck bulge, and his ill-fitting narrow-lapel suit is soaked with sweat. 'This song is for all the people,' he is shouting hoarsely into the mic, beating his hand in the air like a

Elvis Costello - *This Year's Model*: In-depth

seal's flipper, 'who listens to the radio morning, noon and night — and nothing is coming out!' And then he goes into 'Radio, Radio'. His stage act is good, filled with a snarling, thumping intensity. But the album is better, the rhythms worked out in cleaner lines, the dark-dream lyrics more audible. During the second act, Costello is thrown completely and leaves the stage briefly when someone pulls a plug backstage — his stage presence is about as smooth as gravel, nothing like the classic rockers. The era of Chuck Berry and Buddy Holly, in fact, is only history to him."

In March 1978, *It's Only Rock 'N' Roll* reported on a gig that took place on 25th January 1978 at Armadillo World Headquarters in Austin, Texas; "Walking into Austin's Inner Sanctum Records one can see that the Elvis Costello phenomenon has struck hard and fast. They offer gift certificate prizes in their E.C. look-alike contest; they're selling Elvis sweatshirts, gigantic posters of the elfin rock figure hang from the walls and large stand-ups of Elvis aim true at customers waiting to buy tickets to his already sold-out performance for this night at Armadillo World HQ. The Armadillo is jam-packed by eight o'clock and the show doesn't begin for an hour — unusual for Austin where folks are known to saunter in just minutes before the main act steps on stage. Many people have come from San Antonio and surrounding parts to see what could be "the next big thing"... An intense Elvis Costello took the stage, and the first Armadillo crowd in six months was on its feet for the entire concert. With little ado Costello opened his show with 'Welcome To The Working Week', a bit of an analogy of his present situation. 'Now that your picture's in the paper...'. Being the new kid in town is a heavy task but it's also just another job. After a fast rendition of 'Red Shoes' he did 'Miracle Man' about the almost impossible expectations of a lover. Elvis' band is a tightly knit unit that followed his every move. The keyboardist on Vox organ and piano took most of the lead work while Elvis played rhythm and concentrated on lyrics and poses. His show was energetic, taken at a non-stop pace with dedicated playing from the band. The poignant 'Alison', done with Steve Nieve on piano, was followed by Elvis' rock 'n' roll sermonette on the state of radio, 'Radio, Radio'. Elvis lambasted the medium even though he might be 'biting the hand that feeds.' Costello performed the menacing, cinematic, 'Watching The Detectives', with which he pulled the audience into his movie. Elvis did about fifty percent from his LP and fifty percent new material. His personality onstage was not cold and distant as presented in other rock papers. It was definitely business with no time for pauses between numbers, but Elvis certainly kept the spirit and calibre of his performance high throughout. His performance, at times, was reminiscent of a "fire and brimstone" preacher. Costello has the ability to pinpoint his anger at people and situations and problems with laser-like accuracy. Many of the so-called punk groups fail to do this and just flail away at problems without naming them. The sinister 'Less Than Zero' had him more resigned than angry about the problem of British Nazi Oswald Mosley on the BBC, and although the slide guitar work on the stalking, Dylanesque 'Waiting For The End Of The World' was sorely missed it nevertheless hit home. Elvis finished the set with a fast-paced 'Mystery Dance' which lost the finesse of the arrangement on record but was still well-received and had the audience howling with the laughter of recognition. He came back for an encore, after switching guitars, and did 'This Year's Girl' and one other. It was, indeed, one of the finest rock 'n' roll shows ever seen. When Elvis sings his songs of repression, guilt and anger, it is heightened to an even greater degree because of the contradiction of his onstage persona. Somehow, his looks don't seem to go along with what he's trying to say. But, just remember Peter Lorre from the movies and you can begin to understand that Elvis is just the underdog having his day. We're not saying that Elvis Costello is "the next big thing", but he could be. He expresses himself better than any lyricist since Lennon left the scene. You could never dance to Dylan and think about what he was saying, and the Beatles lost it with their broader concepts. Elvis gives the best of both. He's got the moniker and he can wear the crown."

Costello was in high demand. It was considered in *Circus* in February 1978; "He is suddenly much more than a cult figure, this awkward, half-hidden rocker who goes by the name of Elvis Costello. He's made a quick but effective tour from San Francisco to Asbury Park, and his album was selling at the healthy pace of 10,000 copies per week for the first six weeks it was in American stores.

Elvis Costello - *This Year's Model*: In-depth

Elvis has come a long way from the day, earlier this year, when he was arrested for performing an impromptu solo concert in the street. That performance, which came a few hours before his London stage debut, was a well-orchestrated publicity stunt that may or may not have speeded his signing with Columbia Records (who were having a convention inside a hotel while Costello stopped traffic outside). But later at Dingwalls, a local pub, it all came down to Elvis and his group — Peter Thomas, drums, Bruce Thomas, bass, and Steve Nieve, keyboards — and they knocked back the audience with a fast-paced twenty-one song set. For over ninety minutes the band covered rock and roll, reggae, pop and ballads with a spare but insistent sound that connected intimately with a crowd that stood shoulder to shoulder cheering him on. Elvis' singing was marked by a mix of ferocity and control as he ran through barely familiar future album tracks and such remarkable works-in-progress as 'Lipstick Vogue', 'Chelsea', and 'Lip Service'. Despite all the ovations and shrieks of 'Elvis is king,' despite the knocked-kneed stance, pointed-guitar pose, and a passing resemblance to Buddy Holly, Elvis looks the antithesis of a rock star. Yet *My Aim Is True* has gone from being a curiosity item when it was released in the United Kingdom last June to being an FM radio staple here. Well before its US release, it became one of the most-played import records (Stiff) of the past five years. Even without a US record company pushing him, Elvis made his presence felt over the summer as his music generated word-of-mouth buzz that eventually brought him to mass attention. His songs speak for themselves, recounting infidelities and difficult romantic relationships with a sometimes harsh honesty tempered by compassion and wit. As if to underline his fifties lyricism, his music is full of hooks and reference points to classic rock songs of the past two decades. Through all this he maintains his originality, avoiding the clichés and missed punches of comparable artists (from Elliot Murphy on down) in favour of the clarity and insight shown by rock's most gifted tunesmiths (Van Morrison, Graham Parker, Pete Townshend, Bruce Springsteen) with material like the tender 'Alison', 'Waiting For The End Of The World', 'I'm Not Angry', and 'Miracle Man'."

Costello was in high demand to the extent that ticket sale

records were broken at one of the venues he gigged at. It was reported in *Billboard* in January 1978; "Steve Apple, who turned a faltering singles bar into the Hot Club, the city's current punk rock headquarters, reports attendance records broken during a recent two show appearance by England's Elvis Costello. The club holds approximately two hundred and fifty people. 'If we'd had room,' says Apple, 'we could have sold 1,000 tickets easily.' Apple concedes that many visitors to the Hot Club are drawn there initially by curiosity about this new musical phenomenon, 'but about ninety percent of them come back on a regular basis,' he adds. For the Costello engagement, Apple arranged a simulcast on WMRR FM and a remote live broadcast by the local ABC television channel. Both stations reported strong audience response. Apple, who himself manages a "pop New Wave" act called As, concedes that some club owners are reluctant to book New Wave acts for fear of customer violence." The US was keen to welcome Costello throughout 1978.

It was advocated in *Melody Maker* in May 1978; "Without question, the most exciting rock 'n' roll show to hit New York in some time was the triple-bill of Nick Lowe (and Rockpile), Mink DeVille, and Elvis Costello. Costello's *This Year's Model* is one of the hottest-selling albums in New York, and, coupled With Elvis' statement that he won't return to the US until 1979 (we're getting otherwise), an extra midnight show had to be added to the Palladium's schedule, and it too was a near-sellout."

In May 1978, *Creem* reported on a gig that took place on 15th February 1978 at Centre Stage in Milwaukee; "Elvis' defiance and rancour seemed more fitting onstage, where Elvis and The Attractions, his locomoted support unit, launched a fusillade of electrifying and memorable rock tunes. Elvis has been accused of sounding like practically everybody in rock dreams and I'm not about to add to the list. Suffice to say that he delivers the goods. His gruff, evocative vocals fit the mood of today like brass knuckles unleashing vulnerability and rage. Elvis' hour-plus set is jacked-up at a furious, funny-car pace, primed to attack a healthy variety of musical styles, including rockabilly and several hypnotic reggae mood pieces. The highlight: 'Watching The Detectives', a trashy ballad of unrequited lust featuring the immortal Mickey Spillane homage — 'She's filing

Elvis Costello - *This Year's Model*: In-depth

her nails while they're dragging the lake.' His ancient Fender guitar has Elvis punching in at 1958 on the rock 'n' roll time clock. Sporting thick glasses, swept back hair and a baggy gray flannel suit, he looks like a spastic Frankenstein clone of Buddy Holly. Most imitators homogenise their idol; Elvis lobotomises his, whirring around the stage like a runaway, rock-steady robot badly in need of a pair of corrective shoes. The Attractions reinforce his malevolent visage. Their dark glasses and expressionless muskrat faces bring to mind a trio of *Clockwork Orange* droids, ready to pounce on the unsuspecting audience at a moment's notice. Elvis' song intros are masterpieces of comic understatement. 'This song's about London,' he said before a new offering, 'but I'm sure you can apply it to any place you live. It's called 'I Want To Go To Chelsea'' (sic) (pronouncing Chelsea as if it were some sort of horrible mental institute). With Elvis, it is safest to trust the song, not the singer. He boasts that he's 'not angry,' that 'there is no such thing as original sin,' but this is just a facade, an aesthetic chastity belt. He is most comfortable with a hostile audience, who feed on his antagonism and hurl it back in his face. Elvis' post Valentine's Day offering — for all the sweethearts in the crowd — was a cheery ballad called 'Little Triggers'. Last year when playing in front of a bunch of Island Records A&R men, Elvis introduced another new song. 'It's called 'Lip Service',' he said coolly, 'and that's all you're gonna get from me.' Elvis, a black-comic poet of revenge and guilt, has only contempt for sentimental teen-mag romance. 'Everybody loves you so much girl,' he sneers with the braggadocio of early Dylan, 'I don't know how you can stand the strain.' He is jealous of stardom — even the angels want to wear his red shoes. And at twenty-three, his bitterness knows no bounds. 'I'm gonna pay it back,' he sings, spitting in the faces of the stupid music biz hacks who panned his songs one month and lauded them the next. 'I'm gonna pay it back, one of these days.' Now Elvis' day has come. He's not trying to change the world. He's waiting for it to end."

In March 1978, *Melody Maker* reported on a gig that took place on 23rd February at The Ledge, Rutgers University in New Brunswick (at this gig, Willie Alexander opened for Elvis Costello and The Attractions); "There were no seats, but despite strong efforts by both bands, everyone remained seated on the floor. Willie Alexander's set was received with increasing consternation. It was like watching a comedian tell jokes that no one understood... Costello was treated with more familiarity, but it wasn't until thirty or forty minutes into his set that Elvis finally could not handle playing to a bad oil painting anymore. 'This isn't *King Lear*, you know,' he told the crowd of seven hundred. 'We're not in the theatre. Now get up!' And the knee-jerks responded. As usual (it seems). Costello played a wholly different set, in which he not only mixed up the order and selection of songs, but also fiddled with the tempo and vocal arrangements of several of his better recorded numbers. His command of the crowd was evidenced not by the volume of their response but by the moments of total silence he managed to reach when he hushed the band and just baited the fans with a long, expressionless stare. Stand-out numbers in Costello's set were a slow version of 'Less Than Zero', and two new pieces, 'You're Not Another Mouth In The Lipstick Vogue' (sic), and 'This Year's Girl', both rousing rockers. Willie 'Loco' Alexander and Elvis Costello are currently in the midst of a middle-American tour."

Costello's Canadian debut took place on 6th and 7th March 1978 at El Mocambo in Toronto. *Billboard* reported on this in the same month; "Costello draws overflow crowd in Canada debut — Elvis Costello's two-night stint at the El Mocambo created a whirlwind of excitement not seen since The Rolling Stones' appearance at the tame venue last spring. Margaret Trudeau was not seen this time around, but the fortunate three hundred who did make it past the front doors of the club were visibly excited by what they saw and heard. At least 1,000 people were turned away on opening night. More were similarly disappointed the second night but they had been warned in radio and press reports that a first come, first serve policy was in force. Others were content to savour the music at home via a CHUM-FM remote broadcast."

In March 1978, *Melody Maker* reported on a gig that took place on 17th March at Ulster Hall in Belfast; "It is made clear the moment that E.C. and The Attractions bang into 'Waiting For The End Of The World' that seven weeks of intensive US gigging has honed to a vicious edge music that is any way sharper than that of almost any other current rock band. The last time I saw the outfit in action was

Elvis Costello - *This Year's Model*: In-depth

at the Nashville in December and they were lagging slightly, but still putting out more heat than most of us could take without screaming. Tonight the music is slicing across the airwaves in lateral sheets, the sheer impact of which is unimpaired by the inconsistent acoustics. They perform eighteen songs (four of them encores) in something like eighty minutes. It's one relentless rush at the gates of hell, with venom pumped straight off the stage and into the bloodstream. Time was when Elvis moved not at all onstage. He'd stand icy calm and immobile at the storm centre of the musical carnage, maybe flickering an eyelid if he seemed occasionally moved, yelping lyrics to songs of truthful vengeance with all the hypnotic passion he could muster (which was some passion, Harry, believe me!) He's still no Nureyev on the boards, but he's developed this sudden jerking movement that takes him maybe two or three steps either side of the microphone whenever he decides to dash off one of his briefly alarming guitar figures (they're almost too brief to be described as proper solos). He did it first on 'Less Than Zero' and repeated it again on 'The Beat'. That time it conveniently carried him out of the way of a crowd of loonies who staged a pitch invasion, shouted a few obscure slogans, and were hastily dragged away to whatever fate awaits such dramatic interlopers (later identified as members of a band called the Outcasts, who pulled a similar stunt when The Clash played here). Elvis ignores them and gets back on the case via 'This Year's Girl'. On 'Watching The Detectives', Elvis forsakes his guitar to stroll out along some edge of paranoid fright, and 'Pump It Up' and 'You Belong To Me' relax the tension and bring the set to a thrilling conclusion. Still, Belfast is rabid for more, and they perform four exhilarating encores: 'Mystery Dance', 'Miracle Man', the devastating 'Radio, Radio' (one cinch of a single) and a climactic, destructive version of 'I'm Not Angry' that exhausts us all. Then Elvis rips out the lead from his guitar with whiplash reflexes and vanishes."

Not all receptions and reviews were positive. It could either be down to the fact that the eccentricity of Costello's music and performance style wasn't to everyone's taste or perhaps it was the case that considering the number of areas covered across the US tour, maybe not all appearances were well advertised.

Either way, in April 1978, it was reported in the *Detroit Free*

Touring

Press; "Elvis Costello, the New Wave rebel-without-a-cause, made a less than auspicious local debut at the Royal Oak Music Theatre on Saturday night. The sparsely attended shows appeared to be part of a mass conspiracy by Columbia Records, Brass Ring Productions and Elvis himself to keep his career just this side of limbo. Costello, for the unenlightened, is a twenty-three-year-old former computer operator from London who managed to cop the 1977 *Rolling Stone* Album Of The Year Award. His real name is a closely guarded secret — though he appears to be the offspring of some unholy tryst between Woody Allen, Buddy Holly and at least two of The Crickets. This carefully orchestrated aura mystery is doing nobody a favour — not Elvis and certainly not the three hundred plus people who did something less than pack the cavernous auditorium. Questions of artistic purity aside, hype has its uses — such as alerting people to an approaching event. There is no reason for an artist of Elvis' calibre to be playing to three-quarter empty auditoriums except that newspaper and radio advertising were close to non-existent. Part of the problem is Elvis himself. He appears to be angry as hell. He is already semi-legendary for telling a packed house at a CBS convention to 'go fuck yourselves.' 'Elvis just has a hard time relating to people,' a Columbia Records rep said. 'They've put a lid on the press because he can't handle it — he tends to come off very negative.' He was dressed like the ghost of rock and roll past — dark suit, skinny tie, white socks and plain dark loafers — dear lord, he even has acne. Elvis is New Wave only in the vaguest sense — his music defies categorisation. There are traces of Buddy Holly and other late fifties rockers, a dose of mid-sixties British pop the Stones, The Who and such teen rave-ups as Herman's Hermits and more than a little of Bruce Springsteen, the early seventies pseudo-saviour of American rock. Elvis' lyrics are what lift him out of the New Wave genre. They are, in the main, James Dean-style revenge fantasies on a near psychotic level. There is a peculiar, introverted quality to many of them that is chilling — like a man idly twirling a gun, alone, late at night. Elvis is uncompromisingly not nice, though sometimes the tough-guy stance slips and the adolescent fury that fuels his songs seems ridiculously overblown, the reiterated ranting of a grounded teenager. Some day Elvis may sing a ballad. Some day he may even

Elvis Costello - *This Year's Model*: In-depth

fall in love. But, until then, these relentless (and danceable) songs are some of the best music currently coming out of Britain. None of this was really in evidence on Saturday night, with the volume and tempos jacked-up to impossible levels."

In April 1978, *Melody Maker* reported on a gig that took place on 16th April at London's Roundhouse; "It was partly a case of the legend preceding the human being and all his inherent frailties, partly a case of a sloppy backing band, and principally a case of the deified boy himself being unable to sustain the energy on the night. Elvis Costello was a disappointment at London's Roundhouse on Saturday night, and the more I think about it, the more disappointed I feel. But then he had this gigantic reputation to live up to. Honestly, I didn't know what to expect — I hadn't seen Elvis Costello before. But I expected a *lot*. I had a vision of this little bespectacled guy walking out on stage and in one graceful swoop opening his arms to embrace the entire audience and give a unique experience. Elvis didn't have a chance. I really wanted to love him. I'm not too fond of *My Aim Is True*, but *This Year's Model* is one of the best albums released in years. I willed this to take my body apart, and put it back together again, but he only got as far as loosening a few valves. I'm not blaming him; had there not been this holy build up — I liken it to visiting Lourdes sure of a miracle — then I would have stumbled out of the Roundhouse dazzled by a rising new talent. So let's put things in perspective: Elvis Costello is a good writer, singer, performer and artist who needs more time and leeway to become a great one. I'm convinced that to justify his reputation Costello has a few loose ends to tidy up. For a start, his band, The Attractions, who came more into the scheme of his things on *This Year's Model*, need to sharpen up considerably. Perhaps it had to do with the absence of injured bass player Bruce Thomas (Nick Lowe adequately took his place), but I think it goes much deeper than that. The Attractions never actually felt comfortable. Steve Nieve's keyboard playing at times uneasily confronted Elvis' songs rather than complementing them, while drummer Pete Thomas never helped the band swing, often bludgeoning his way through the set."

The review continued; "All this is, of course, relative to Costello's performance and might partially explain why he didn't

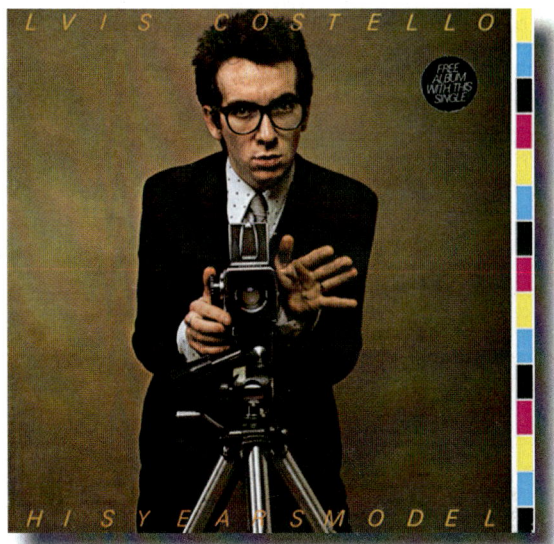

The first 5,000 copies of the album came with a sticker on the front cover and included a freebie single. The tracks included were: 'Stranger In The House' / 'Neat, Neat, Neat'
The CMYK (Cyan, Magenta, Yellow and Black, the printing primary colours) colour band appears to be unique to the UK and… Finland!

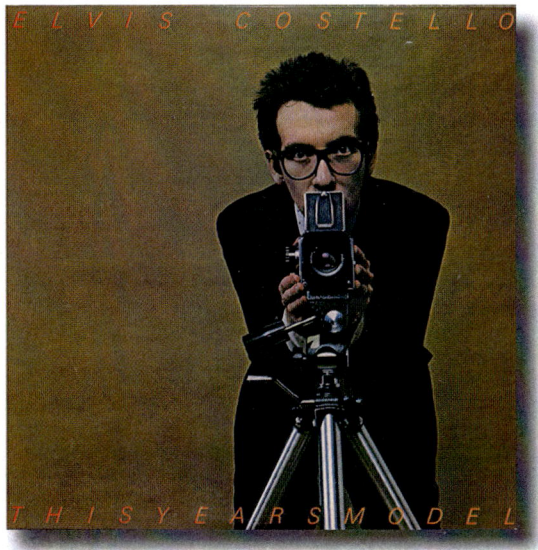

Around the globe however, the covers varied significantly. Different photos were used, as was the case with the US version shown here.

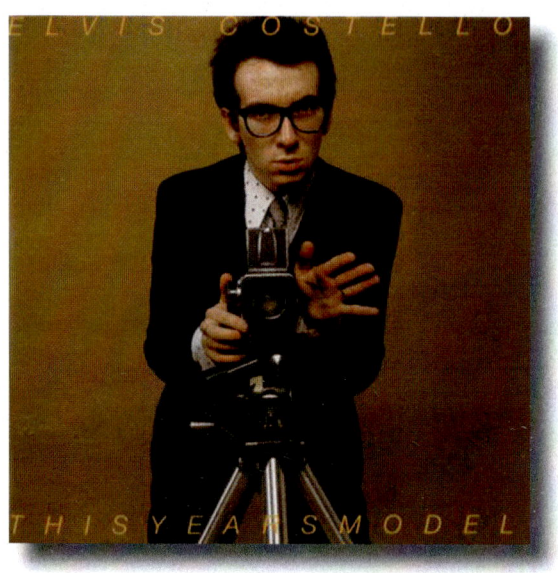

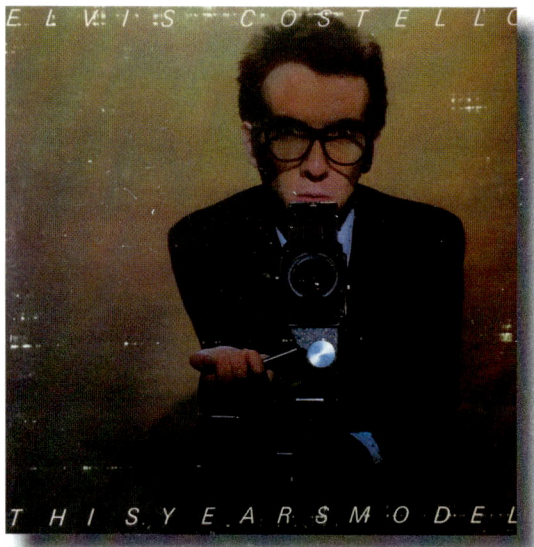

More cover variations. The South African version has the same photo as the UK but no colour bar. In Scandinavia (except Finland) they used a completely different photo altogether.

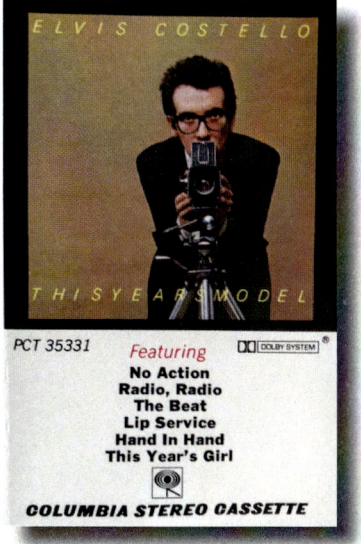

The US 8-track and cassette versions.

UK

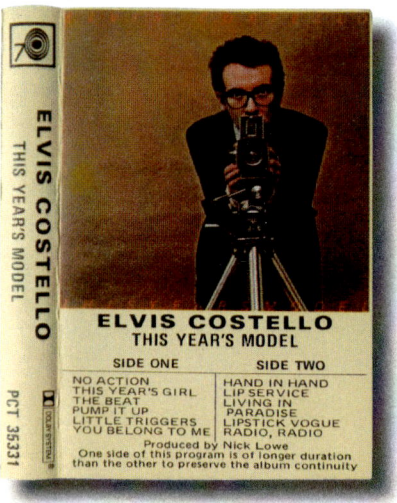

Canada

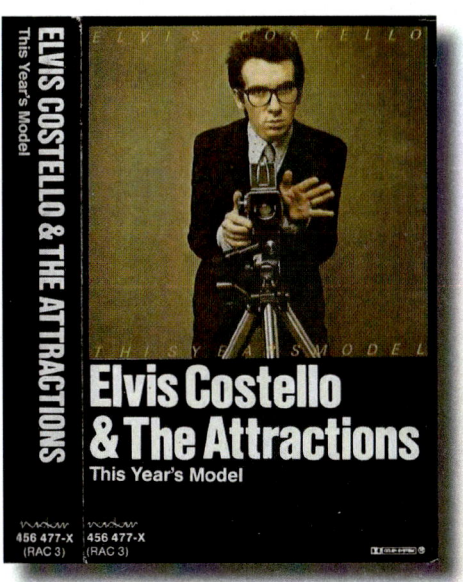

Germany

Scandinavia

More cassette variations for the avid collectors.

UK

USA

As well as the cover variations, the album was released on numerous labels around the world.

Scandinavia

Greece

UK, 1980 reissue

Australia, 1987 reissue

settle down. After literally stunning the Roundhouse into silence during his all-too-brief acoustic set (only three numbers) and racing through songs with The Attractions, he suddenly and inexplicably sagged around the middle, to only partially recover towards the end. But let's not forget the magical moments when he did connect, those incredible times when Costello and his audience physically joined. For me it was during 'This Year's Girl'. There was this slight, baggy-suited figure on stage commanding his followers, and they religiously mouthed the lyrics. It was a moment to savour and one that sent a couple of tingling vibrations up my spine. I doubt if the audience will agree with my reservations. They cheered deliriously at the end and brought Costello and The Attractions back for a rocking finale with 'Pump It Up' before Nick Lowe took stage centre to sing (badly) 'Breaking Glass' and 'Heart Of The City'. By this time, The Rumour's Martin Belmont had joined the entourage and uncovered another little flaw. Costello could use a rhythm guitarist to beef up the sound."

Regarding the absence of Bruce Thomas, an injury to his right hand had occurred in a dressing room at Manchester Rafters. *Melody Maker* had reported on it the previous week. The bassist had to have eighteen stitches in his hand after an accident with a broken bottle. No other information was provided.

The previous night's performance at the Roundhouse was reviewed in *New Musical Express* that month; "The roadies set up The Attractions' complete stage gear, so it was clear that a replacement for Bruce Thomas had been found, but no one was letting on as to the identity of the mystery bassist — it seemed that Elvis wanted to keep the punters guessing. Then suddenly, completely unannounced (oh, the drama of it all!), Elvis runs on alone, bows(!), stares at the crowd, and starts to play a song called, I think, 'She'll Be The One', on his guitar. The song over, he pauses to say 'Good evening. How are you?' to smile even, before playing 'Chemistry Class'. Still no mention of the replacement bassist, until he introduces Pete Thomas and Steve Nieve and then... is it? ... no, but it can't be... yes it is — Nick Lowe, who proceeds to play perfectly sound bass throughout the set. The last time I saw Elvis was in August of last year when he was still playing weekly gigs at the Nashville. He was good, sure, but

Elvis Costello - *This Year's Model*: In-depth

I felt that he was performing at rather than for, the audience. No such qualms this time however. He immediately seemed more confident and relaxed, no doubt the effect of assorted Stiff and American tours, but was still just as charismatic a performer. The sound was better too, so I could hear the keyboards properly and Steve Nieve, his gaunt features offset by a pair of round shades so that he looked like nothing so much as some giant insect, proved, with only an electric piano and a Vox Continental, how utterly unnecessary synthesisers are (for all their supposed versatility). There were times when The Attractions could have been accused of over-speeding so it was the slower numbers that tended to stand out — 'Waiting For The End Of The World', 'Less Than Zero', and even 'Chelsea' all made their studio counterparts sound, well, a little tame. An agreeable surprise also to hear The Attractions' version of 'Alison' not as poignant as the one which graces the grooves of *My Aim Is True* but I suppose that's asking too much, and in an extended 'Watching The Detectives' Elvis' uneasy listening became uneasier still. They were called back for 'Mystery Dance' with Phil Lynott on bass, who obliged with one clenched-fist salute as he left the stage, but there was no way the crowd was going to let them off a second encore so Elvis returned, looking somewhat chuffed at his reception, and explained that they didn't know any more songs ('I'm Not Angry', 'Lipstick Vogue', and 'Night Rally' were all conspicuous by their absence from the set, but credit where it's due — Basher had performed admirably) so Nick was going to sing 'Heart Of The City', and so he did. And that was it. Probably not the best gig Elvis and The Attractions have ever played but, considering the circumstances, still worthy of the highest praise and good enough to make monkeys of most other bands. I didn't yawn once."

The anthemic nature of 'Pump It Up' leant itself to a crazed audience. Pogoing springs to mind here. In April 1978, a concert goer's experience was printed in the reader's letter section of *Melody Maker*; "Last Saturday night I went to see Elvis Costello at Bracknell. He and The Attractions were tremendous, if far too loud for comfort and clarity. However, we all knew he would be great and this does not warrant the effort of me sitting down and scrawling on paper. The audience does! I am a boring old fart of twenty four, have been to many concerts over the last eight years or so and have never come across a crowd like it. Normally at concerts when people are standing and dancing, it tends to be hot, crowded and vaguely uncomfortable. Furthermore, the attitude, as a rule, is one of 'be nice to people and they'll be nice to you.' There is a cheerful atmosphere built on camaraderie in adverse circumstances. Not this time. The Mickey Jupp Band were support and while they were playing, those of us at the front had a good view and could dance happily if we chose to. As soon as the band filed off, however, all the Elvis Costello fans started to push forwards and in at the side so that we barely had room to breathe and were gradually forced backwards by the weight of numbers of totally selfish and inconsiderate school kid punks. Then the pogoing commenced and I noticed several interesting things about it. Firstly, it seems to have nothing at all to do with dancing; it is more an expression of hipness, to use an old expression. Due to its nature, it is a very exerting way of passing one's time. This means that at the start everyone pogos madly until they get knackered. Then they gradually stop, have a rest and then look around them anxiously until one brave boy gives a half-hearted leap. This seems to fill them all with confidence and they all set off again. Very strange. However, you'll be pleased to know that pogoing does have a practical use and that is getting to the front, even when you have come in late. The theory is, I suppose, that if one takes a run up and leaps forward into the air it is easier to push a body aside and get in front of it, especially if the object body is also in mid-air at the time. If it is not, it soon steps backwards to examine its blackening toenails through its Hush Puppies when one lands on its toes. This constant pushing and damaging of other people's bodies does not lend itself to an atmosphere of conviviality. Anyway, both bands were great and a bargain at £1.80, so well done, Elvis, Mickey and the tour organisers. But that audience...!"

Notably, Costello seemed to be appreciative of a positive audience response. He was quoted in *It's Only Rock 'N' Roll* in June 1978; "I really love Texas out of the whole US. The audiences are good to us here. I love the music scene in Austin, because there's so much good music here. We're thinking of moving here. We wouldn't actually live here. But we'd use it as a stop-over place to stay and

Elvis Costello - *This Year's Model*: In-depth

store our equipment. I like the wide-open countryside. We'd like to base ourselves here to get away from LA and New York. We'd like a place in between the two and to record in one or the other. But the people are so burnt-out in those places." When asked if he preferred playing in larger halls, Costello was quoted in the same feature; "No, we need to get back to playing bar music. People are more reserved when they go to a concert than they are in a small club. I understand why the Stones picked the El Mocambo club to record in. It has a great feel to the acoustics."

A performance that took place on 23rd May 1978 at the Municipal Auditorium in Austin, Texas was reviewed in *It's Only Rock 'N' Roll* in June 1978; "It was a perfect triple bill. Elvis Costello, the "angry young man" of the New Wave; his producer and neo-popstar Nick Lowe; and sandwiched between, the original Spanish Johnny, Willy 'Mink' DeVille. Unfortunately the show was only about two-thirds sold out. When it began at 7:30 there were perhaps one hundred people in the audience. A few hundred more sauntered in during Nick Lowe's opening set but most of the crowd missed some excellent rock 'n' pop from Lowe and his backup band Rockpile. Even though the show wasn't a sellout, the crowd was ferocious in its love for Elvis. As the houselights dimmed, Elvis and The Attractions, with instruments in-hand, hit the stage like bank robbers running for a getaway car. The bespectacled Elvis was a stark figure wearing a white untucked shirt. Gone was his rummage sale jacket and tie. Gone too was the nervousness and ill-at-ease manner from the first time he'd played Austin back in February. Gone too was the thatched-hair which was now fashionably longer. But the tension was still there. Even though he seemed looser it was easy to see that he was still a tightly-coiled steel spring that could lash out at any moment. With a 'Wipeout' drum intro Elvis & Co. ran through a frenetically-paced 'Mystery Dance'. He looked truly amazed at the reaction as girls screamed and clamoured for his body. Elvis is a well-known misogynist, at least in song, and that type of response seemed more in-place for Gino Vannelli. Elvis is also an intellectual songwriter and there were many who were actually singing along with his complex lyrics. Elvis didn't wait for applause but raced right into 'Pump It Up' and 'Waiting For The End Of The World' in tandem. 'End Of The World' was taken at breakneck speed and lost all the finesse and the loping rhythm the original has. The group blew through the Who-like 'No Action' like they were on speed, and like the other songs before it the lyrics were nearly indecipherable. 'Less Than Zero' was performed in a listless manner but was saved by Steve Nieve's organ solo which sounded like a combination of 'La Bamba' and 'Telstar'. Serious roller rink music."

The review continued; "The crowd was surging around the stage as security guards began telling individuals to take their seats and even shoving others who wouldn't move back. Elvis was plainly peeved at this reaction from the guards. He shouted into the mic, 'It's beginning to look like a fucking prison camp up here! I don't know about you but I wouldn't like someone in a uniform with a big stick to push me around!' With those words a near riot broke out as most fans in their seats reacted with words in kind. But most of the crowd returned to their seats for the time being. Elvis then performed a country-western tune, 'Stranger In The House'. When Elvis jumped into 'Red Shoes' the emotion seemed to finally come through in his singing like it hadn't in his previous songs. The band ran through 'This Year's Girl', 'Miracle Man' and 'Lip Service'. Elvis was manic in his gesturing and minimal guitar playing but the band worked as if it was all of a piece. They were so tight a unit that if Elvis sneezed the rest said Gesundheit! Elvis and The Attractions performed a new ballad, 'Party Girl'. 'Watching The Detectives', Elvis' bizarre movie-in-song, was next and with Pete Thomas' spectacular reggae drum work and the spooky lead guitar line, it pulled the audience all the way into Costello's private world. 'Detectives' is clearly Elvis' most intriguing song and the performance was the show's tour de force. E.C. & Co. then ran through the frenzied 'The Beat' with its line, 'I don't wanna be your lover, I just wanna be your victim,' aimed directly at the audience. 'This next tune is off my album *My Aim Is True*,' Elvis told the fans before slipping into the bittersweet ballad 'Alison'. Elvis was in particularly fine voice and the heart-wrenching lyrics came across truer than ever. 'You Belong To Me' had the crowd dancing in the aisles again and then marching towards the stage as Elvis shot the finger at them, saying, 'I hope this'll get a bit of life into you! If you don't know what's wrong with

Elvis Costello - *This Year's Model*: In-depth

radio, you don't know what's wrong with you!' Then he attacked the crowd with 'Radio, Radio', his Molotov cocktail hurled at the medium. After that song Elvis and his gang sprinted offstage as the crowd gave them a standing ovation. Minutes later they came back and launched into '(I Don't Want To Go To) Chelsea'. Elvis played more guitar in this tune over the machine gun-like drumming and the sneaking bass line. After they received a second encore they drove like a locomotive through 'Lipstick Vogue'. On 'I'm Not Angry' Elvis aimed his guitar at the crowd like a machine gun. They answered him on the chorus line screaming 'I'm Not Angry'! Finally Elvis stalked offstage followed by his group. He'd again delivered a riveting and electrifying performance."

Elvis Costello and The Attractions played as the opening act for Mink DeVille on May 30th 1978 at the Santa Monica Civic Auditorium in California. The performance was reviewed in *Cash Box* in June 1978; "It is unfortunate that a poor sound system slightly tarnished what otherwise would have been a brilliant evening of contemporary rock 'n' roll by three of the best acts spawned in the New Wave. Elvis Costello, who has already established himself as a highly-intense, often "angry" performer, demonstrated the most pronounced reaction to the sound problem by throwing his guitar offstage several times and finally kicking over one of the offending amplifiers. While he was playing, however, there was no stopping him. In less than a year, Costello has created one of the most impressive bodies of work perhaps to come out of the 1970s. His songs contain the powerful point of view and individuality reserved for the most valuable artists. As a performer, he has moved beyond the stiffness he sometimes displayed during his debut here last fall. Now he is more apt to move around the stage and make use of movements, the most effective of which were some exaggerated hands-to-head thrusts. And even though his *This Year's Model* album has only been out a short time, Elvis continues to supplement his shows with healthy doses of material not found on his two albums. It is easy to zero in on the anger and frustration in his songs (while bypassing the humour and satire), but then a big part of Elvis' message is missed. He is looking from a new vantage point, so his lyrics don't simply rehash the same frustration voiced by The Rolling Stones and Bob Dylan ten

Touring

years ago or Elvis Presley and Eddie Cochran ten years before that. His hostility is not just directed at an overly-technological society, but more specifically at a mass media-dominated culture and a new generation raised totally in that media-laden environment. Costello is saying. 'Don't trust celebrities — including myself.' This isn't to say an Elvis Costello concert isn't fun, as his songs musically blend these themes with the exuberance and infectiousness of 1950s and 1960s pop. Not to mention clever lighting tricks which turned Elvis green with envy during 'Alison' and red with rage for 'Living In Paradise'."

From a different perspective, in June 1978, the *Los Angeles Times* reported on the same gig that took place on 30th May at the Santa Monica Civic Auditorium; "Elvis Costello is one of rock's most captivating new arrivals, but the English singer-songwriter hasn't got the best sense of timing. After complaining last weekend about the media's preoccupation with angry-young-man undercurrents in his music and manner, Costello threw a tantrum Tuesday night at the Santa Monica Civic Auditorium. Apparently angered by equipment problems that stripped the music of some power, the twenty-three-year-old rocker hurled his guitar down, kicked over an amplifier and stomped off the stage about forty minutes into the show. But the audience refused to leave. Not even the turning on of the house lights and, eventually, the closing of the stage curtain stopped the cheers from those hoping to lure Costello back for another try. After several minutes, he and his Attractions band did return, but the equipment continued to give him problems. Midway through the second encore number, Costello again flung the guitar. Prowling the stage with a tense, almost explosive air, he finished the song and then left. Adding to the strange, maniacal mood, the band's Bruce Thomas threw his bass on top of the drums, leaving the instruments in a tangle. This time the curtain closed for good. The incident will no doubt serve as a colourful anecdote for Costello enthusiasts, but it also left a dark, disorienting aftermath to what otherwise was a stirring concert hall debut here for the singer. Far more confident and convincing a performer than his Whisky appearance last November, Costello bristled with energy and purpose, often punctuating the lyrics with dramatic hand movements. Without resorting to the primitive,

Elvis Costello - *This Year's Model*: In-depth

safety-pinned attire or often self-conscious hostility of the British punk movement, Costello does reflect the relentless determination of that rock contingent."

The review continued; "He could benefit from a second guitarist to give his four-piece outfit's music variety and punch, but his lyrics are among the most finely honed and involving of anyone in rock, and the overall sound is enticing. Despite an intensity and bite that provide a frequent angry backdrop, the music is a richly fulfilling blend of humour, compassion and desire. 'Mystery Dance', which opened the show, is a light-hearted look at awkward sexual awakening. 'This Year's Girl' is a tender look at the victims of a trendy, values-lacking society. 'Red Shoes' is a sly, mocking jab at self-pity which includes a line that perhaps best summarises Costello's somewhat bittersweet, recovery-from-life's-pain approach: 'Well, I used to be disgusted...'. Beyond the starkness of his mostly stern stage stance, there's a celebratory, we-can-pull-through-the-problems-together tone to Costello's music. As with most superior artists, there's an uplifting message behind the glimpses of disappointment and doubt. That's why the temper display near the end of the hour set was self-destructive. Rather than building toward an exhilarating climax, Costello short-circuited the process, leaving the incident rather than the music as the final impression. With the equipment problems presumably corrected, Costello will have more chances this week to build that more satisfying momentum. His concerts tonight at Long Beach's Millikan High School and Sunday at Hollywood High School are sold out, but some tickets are still available for Friday's show at UC Santa Barbara's Robertson Gym."

In June 1978, *Circus* reported on one of his live performances; "It's 1:30am in the Bootlegger Lounge in Syracuse, NY. Elvis Costello, the one with the owlish stare and the spitting mad vocals, the man whose songs may be the worst thing that's happened to feminism since Jack the Ripper, is leaning solicitously towards an elegant brunette in a low-cut black dress. Around the corner is the Landmark Theatre, a rococo movie palace where Elvis had berated and rocked a full house into a frenzy two hours before. He had run through some of the nastier cuts from his second Columbia album, *This Year's Model*, ending with a bellowing encore version of 'I'm Not Angry' from last year's debut, *My Aim Is True*. 'There'd better be some movin' around,' Costello had threatened, and he was getting some. He was making the crowd — 'Citizens of Syracuse', he'd called them — shout out the last word of the song's refrain. Five, six, ten, twelve, thirteen, fourteen, more times, till nobody was counting as Elvis shook his fist. Straightjacketed in a gabardine sportscoat and black shirt, running through the manual of arms with his guitar as he leaned over it to throttle the mic, dropping to his knees on 'You Belong To Me', Elvis was earning his money. Not that he had to — his first record sold over 300,000 copies, and *This Year's Model* is well on its way to eclipsing it. But his present US tour, which has just finished up on the West Coast after a clockwise sweep through the country, is vindication for Elvis and his producer — fellow-performer Nick Lowe. And they are making sure to stuff their brand of rock and roll deep into the US craw... The onstage Elvis puts the lyrics across even more heatedly than the recorded one. In Syracuse, he delivered a series of indignant stabs at womankind. 'This Year's Girl', for example, feels like a ride on a carousel that's slipped its drive chain as Elvis excoriates Farrah Fawcett-Majors types: 'See her picture in a thousand places...' Elvis does his countrified quickie-single, 'Stranger In The House', and manages to leave tearstains all over the stage he has just belted '(I Don't Want To Go To) Chelsea' from. 'Sometimes I think that love is just a tumour,' sings Elvis on 'Lipstick Vogue', as he spreads his fingers across his chest, 'You've got to cut it out.' He flings his hand sideways, a gesture as abrupt as one he makes later — flipping the bird to a cheering audience. For all the adoration that pours over him, Elvis still seems to work off the nasty half of a love-hate relationship with crowds. Playing the Whiskey in LA, Elvis got perturbed by a heckler who was part of a milling pack just below the stage. He poured a glass of coke on the offender's head, and, getting a splash of beer in return, smashed the glass on his mic stand and wiggled it before him. Not exactly your "it's-really-great-to-be-here" routine... Elvis Costello, then, is definitely this year's model for a rock star. Tougher than punk, more touching than MOR, a better beat than disco — and all with integrity. The kind of integrity that approaches rage, and makes for crashing, cathartic rock and roll concerts."

Costello made a guest appearance with Delbert McClinton on

Elvis Costello - *This Year's Model*: In-depth

25th July 1978 at Lone Star Café in New York. It was reported on in *Circus* in September 1978 under the heading of "Elvis jams with honky tonk heroes"; "For a guy who's not exactly a star yet, honky tonk bluesman Delbert McClinton sure attracts more than his share of same whenever he plays New York City. On his most recent visit to the Apple's Lone Star Cafe — a citybilly C&W hangout — Delbert was joined onstage by R&B songwriting legend Otis Blackwell for a duet on 'Don't Be Cruel' (one of the classics Blackwell penned for Elvis Presley), and then both men were joined by New Wave iconoclast Elvis Costello (who first sat in with McClinton in a Dallas roadhouse last year) for a blues jam that lasted well into the a.m."

It was during November that the tour went to Japan. When asked about what was his first trip there in 1978, Costello was quoted in *The Japan Times* in September 2016; "Ah, our attempt to get ourselves in the papers. Nobody took any notice. It just goes to show what would make the papers in England wouldn't make a ripple in Japan. Too unprecedented I guess! We thought we'd be hauled away and it would be a fantastic scandal and that's how we'd make our name. But it didn't work out that way." (The band had dressed like Japanese schoolboys in Nehru jackets with brass buttons. They hired a truck, drove it through Tokyo's ritzy Ginza district playing music as loudly as the amplification would allow whilst throwing their records at the gathering crowds). It is this kind of hindsight that suggests that maybe, outside of the music itself, quite a lot was done in the lexicon of publicity stunts at the time.

In December 1978, *Cash Box* reported on the troublesome events following Costello's gig that took place on 3rd December in Sydney's Regent Theatre; "Sydney rock fans turned their fury on the Regent Theatre after Elvis Costello failed to give them an encore. Costello, Britain's top New Wave performer, would not come back on stage after a show of less than sixty minutes because he said the audience reaction was 'too mechanical.' The initial cheers from the two hundred plus crowd turned into boos and catcalls when it became clear Costello was not coming back on stage. Next, pieces of the seats started hurtling towards the stage, first from the circle area and then from the stalls. Announcements over the public address system were made, asking the crowd to disperse peacefully or all other Costello concerts would be cancelled. The crowd then began to leave the theatre amid chants of 'Elvis loves his money' and 'Costello is a capitalist.' Several hundred people gathered outside the theatre, ripping Elvis posters from the entrance."

The event was corroborated in *Melody Maker* in the same month. It was reported that Costello apparently screamed to his manager to shield him from the photographers, one of whom he shouted at, "Who the fucking hell do you think you are?"

In December 1978, *Melody Maker* reviewed a gig that took place in the same month at the Dominion Theatre in London; "What is it about Elvis Costello that makes us want to know about his home life? And what is it that makes him cover his traces with such determination? In his poem, *The Hollow Men*, T.S. Eliot wrote of 'Paralysed force, gesture without motion' — suggesting a kind of emotional impotence which may be what Costello is trying, through his red-raw songs and wilfully unpredictable performances, to overcome. Without access to his analyst's log, I couldn't say. It's possible, of course, that Costello's public personality is a careful fabrication (and that possibility makes the riddle more exquisite). But, real or imagined, his character has such a welcome definition and curious integrity that in the end the hypotheses don't matter. He's not yet a very reliable performer. The last song of the regular set at Monday's show (the first of his pre-Christmas season) was 'Pump It Up': drummer Pete Thomas played the first chorus somewhat faster than Costello chose to sing it, so that the drums finished the chorus a half-bar ahead of Elvis. This led to recriminatory scowls all round, and bassist Bruce Thomas was so affected that he appeared to kick his mic-stand into the photographers' pit. The sour suggestion of impending mayhem wasn't dispelled until the song's end, and it took a dynamite encore — 'Radio, Radio' — to suppress the neurosis. Until 'Pump It Up', the set had built from an exciting but somewhat sloppy opening with 'Peace Love And Understanding' and 'Red Shoes' (not a good juxtaposition, as both songs depend for added kick on unison triplet fills) through a careful mixture of familiar songs and pieces from the forthcoming album. Costello's songs don't really take shape until they're heard on record, so it's hard to assess the eventual impact of the likes of 'Accidents Will Happen',

Elvis Costello - *This Year's Model*: In-depth

'Oliver's Army', and something that might be called 'Dancing Slowly'. The balance, with Steve Nieve's sharp organ camouflaging Costello's words, militated against analysis — which may be what Elvis wants, but it does deprive us of the jewelled details which stud his best songs. The thematically-linked trilogy of 'Chelsea', a coruscating 'Lipstick Vogue' (his greatest song holder in perpetuity of the 'Positively 4th Street' Memorial Award), and 'This Year's Girl' was magnificent, though, as was 'Watching The Detectives', greatly enhanced by clever lighting which created the illusion that Elvis was sitting at home watching TV, the cathode rays reflected on his face."

After a year of very mixed gig reviews — some dominated by tales of confrontation, others portraying a very together band in Elvis Costello and The Attractions — it wasn't long after that Costello's third album would be released. *This Year's Model* and the gigs that followed its release had certainly made an indelible mark.

Chapter Four
A Legacy

This Year's Model was one of many highlights in Elvis Costello's career. The album captured a relevant social commentary reflective of the time in which it was made in a way that wasn't preachy. Rather than advocating for smashing things up and destroying them, with *This Year's Model*, Costello offered a witty commentary across a range of themes and ideas. Amongst that, the album is short, snappy and musically accessible without filler — every track offers something worthwhile. Such was the success and indeed, relevance of *This Year's Model* in 1978 that it was very visible in the music press (so much so that I have managed to source an immense number of reviews. I have endeavoured to include them all in this book because they all offer a worthwhile insight in terms of how the album was perceived overall as well as all of the interesting quirks that each reviewer picked up on — essentially I consider them all to be worthy of archiving here).

This Year's Model was reviewed in *Sounds* in March 1978; "The insult that made a man out of Mac(manus). As runs the hype: get sand kicked in your face (or whatever), keep on punching your computer, night time write songs pouring it all out, fix up some Hank B Marvin hornrims, in a greater display of perverse bravado than he ever managed, call yourself Elvis (and get away with it), recreate yourself, via mystique a-go-go, become: "star". Hypes usually leave out the essential thing in the effort to make the subject at once "next door" and "unreachable" — the talent. Costello has it. And now he's successful, the anger also, and the drive to maintain momentum, to ram that sand right down the guy's throat. No standing still, no resting on past laurels; this album is the quantum leap that you would hope for over *My Aim Is True* (but that usually you'd fail to get) in most every respect bar the material, which is merely consistent.

Elvis Costello - *This Year's Model*: In-depth

Costello and The Attractions are probably, along with the American variant Blondie, the best sixties synthesists going: sixties traces/riffs, like the 'Watcha Gonna Do 'Bout It'/'The Last Time' match of 'You Belong To Me', blatant or otherwise, like the 'Summer Holiday' steal on 'The Beat', fill the album. What matters here (and elsewhere) is the overall impression of ease in which the sources are assimilated, and remoulded into a powerful, attractive, and contemporary whole. Take 'The Beat' already mentioned. Okay: starting with the 'Summer Holiday' lyrical and musical cop, The Attractions and Elvis mix that in with a reggae backbeat, the pun of the title — 'Beat' as in police walking around looking for you as well as what you twitch to — and lyrics like: 'See your friends...' or 'I don't wanna be your ...' This is a fair example of the technique at work throughout the album — except for the slower and, in comparison, less inventive 'Little Triggers' a generousness of lyrical and musical ideas that provides the necessary foil for the bitterness and frequent meanness of the lyrical content. Staples of the sound at once at the ready and The Mysterians' organ and angular chiming guitar bursts throughout. The Attractions are spare yet full — no excess flash, no redundant padding — and impressively tight. And, bearing in mind the simple limitations of numbers, varied. Fave instrumental moments are the massive bass in 'Lip Service', the Al Kooper organ in 'This Year's Girl', the slapped disco drum of 'Pump It Up', the instrumental break in 'Lipstick Vogue' where the verse suddenly switches to a gradual climax of massed guitar, switching again flash fast to pounding drums. The more you listen, the more there is. 'Sometimes I think love is just a tumour...': Costello's lyrics abound in puns, throwaway images — sometimes Dylan through Springsteen in their intensity, bitterness and crammed delivery. The lyrics of 'Lipstick Vogue' from which the above, spill over, burst out of the verses, driven on by drums. 'Living In Paradise' has Elvis getting right down to serious peeping in the middle of economic "plenty"; 'Later in the evening when arrangements are made...' You might have the technology but people don't change, do they? Sometimes, in its accuracy in pinpointing targets and hitting them, and in the choice of target ('Chelsea'), this album reminds of nothing so much as a 1978 *Aftermath*. And the misogyny: at least on occasions Elvis has the grace to make clear it's a two-way process and he's at fault. Just wanna be your victim.

A Legacy

In these days of the renaissance of the potboiler this is an excellent soon-to-be-popular album. Contemporary in intensity, pace and feel — the "new" wave or not question being irrelevant by now — and popular potentially — as in "good strong material well played" — without pandering. It's difficult to fault. Personally these ears find Elvis less than loveable, let alone likeable, but that's not what he deals in. 'Sometimes I almost feel just like a human being.' Too bitter? He nevertheless commands respect. And, what's rare these days in a popular performer, he lets the outside world in."

The album was reviewed in *Melody Maker* in March 1978; "*This Year's Model* — and it's difficult to believe from the maturity of the writing and the performance that it's only The Man's second album! — is an achievement so comprehensive, so inspired, that it exhausts superlatives. It promotes its author to the foremost ranks of contemporary rock writers. Clear out of sight of most of his rivals and comparisons (so long, Bruce baby), Elvis Costello's prodigious talent, we can see in retrospect, was only superficially exposed on his first album. While it is true that *Aim*'s specific themes of revenge, jealousy, infidelity, deceit and betrayal are central to this album's most powerful songs — 'Lip Service', 'Lipstick Vogue' and 'Living In Paradise' — these obsessions are forced even more ruthlessly into the spotlight. And, running parallel to these preoccupations, is the vague paranoia and unease of 'The Beat' and 'Night Rally' which hardens to vicious attack on '(I Don't Want To Go To) Chelsea', a virulent indictment of the superficialities of style and fashion: 'Everybody has new orders...' Nick Lowe's production is easily his finest hour, a firm but sympathetic treatment of the songs, and embellishments that are carefully considered. It brings Elvis' sneering vocal into dramatic close-up — his voice throughout has tremendous presence — as The Attractions, with characteristic razorblade cool, slice across the mix. The themes of infidelity and humiliation are pursued with relentless vigour and imagination. 'Hand In Hand' — which has a backward tape fade-in redolent of 10cc and a gorgeously rich and infectious melody — seems to propose love as a criminal conspiracy: ('Don't ask me to apologise...'). The extraordinary 'Living In Paradise' is set against a neurotic calypso backdrop, with Elvis phrasing his lyrics with a flippant, disquieting glee. The song unfolds as an epic of suspicion, jealousy and revenge, replete with the kind of dangerous

Elvis Costello - *This Year's Model*: In-depth

images that elevated 'I'm Not Angry' to such chilling peaks: 'Later in the evening when the arrangements are made. I'll be at the keyhole outside your bedroom door,' sings Elvis, voice twitching and kicking over the jerking rhythm. 'You think that I don't know the boy that you're touching / but I'll be at the video and I will be watching.' Sex is again the theme of 'This Year's Girl', a brilliant exposition of the hypocrisy that can be provoked by the exploitation of unattainable objects. Elvis flicks off taut guitar sequences over Steve Nieve's swirling keyboard shrouds and a central percussion motif that exaggerates the mounting tension."

The review continued; "A similar abrasiveness characterises the paranoid rush of the epic 'The Beat', which follows. The fierce tango arrangement has been retained from the live prototype that Elvis has been performing since he formed The Attractions, but the fury has been tempered in favour of a more insidious pulse. Steve Nieve's icy keyboard interpolations (imagine a crazed hybrid of Garth Hudson and Can's Irmin Schmidt, if you can) shiver nervously behind Elvis's alarm-central lyrics. The standard of the writing, where the penetration of the language matches the vaulting hysteria of the performance, is relaxed only twice — midway through side one — with 'Pump It Up' and 'Little Triggers'. The former is a routine rocker (I'm sure Nick Lowe told me that this is one of the tracks on which The Clash's Mick Jones played — 'to Keef it up' — but he's not much in evidence), while 'Triggers' employs an overly familiar ballad scheme with a predictable melody, a fault that is not overcome by the rather intriguing lyrics. Still, things are quickly whacked back into shape with 'You Belong To Me', which brings the side to a roaring conclusion, and by the complete magnificence of side two which includes 'Hand In Hand'. 'Chelsea' — dealt with already — as well as 'Lip Service,' 'Lipstick Vogue' and the masterful 'Night Rally'. 'Lip Service' features an especially deft Lowe production job, with acoustic guitars skating beneath Elvis' lead vocal and handclaps punctuating the chorus. 'Lipstick Vogue' is altogether more violent, with Pete Thomas' drums careening from speaker to speaker (here recalling the intro to the live version of 'Mystery Dance'), and Elvis' scatter-chord guitar knocking the song along at a slashing pace. The arrangement is unusually powerful and imaginative. The instruments, having hit one furious-peak, fall away behind Elvis, then rise again to a final crescendo so deranged that this listener is left quite breathless. Elvis and Basher, however, have left until last the album's most lethal broadside. 'Night Rally' is a disturbing comment upon the popularity and potential menace of the National Front that achieves its resonance not from any sensational sloganeering but from the genuine apprehension conveyed by Lowe's discreet atmosphere of impending disaster and Elvis' desolate lyric: 'They're putting all your names in the forbidden book...' It is fitting that such an important song concludes such an impressive album. *This Year's Model*. This Year's Masterpiece. The best thing I've heard since the last best thing I heard. Etc. Etc. Etc."

This Year's Model was reviewed in *Cash Box* in April 1978; "Elvis Costello so far has produced the highest yield of any of England's New Wave crop imported to our shores. His second album is every bit the equal of his superb debut LP, enabling Costello to transcend the early comparisons to Graham Parker and Bruce Springsteen and emerge with an identity all his own. Key to that image is his stance against the shallowness of human character which is happening too much in today's mechanised, passionless society. For AOR and top forty."

It was reviewed in the *Los Angeles Times* in May 1978; "With his horn-rimmed glasses and mild-mannered reporter appearance, Costello doesn't look much like a rock star. But his music is right in step with the classic rock pulse. His vocals bristle with a conviction and bite that we rarely find in rock in the seventies. Thanks to crisper production touches, *Model* with its tales of frustration and desire is even more potent than last year's solid *My Aim Is True*. There's a sensual urgency to 'Pump It Up' that should make the song a show-stopper live, and Costello's taunting 'Radio, Radio' is a call to arms that deserves the cheers of anyone who is disillusioned with the dreariness of top forty radio."

In April 1978, the *Los Angeles Times* had reviewed *This Year's Model* more extensively; "Punk is out. Power Pop is in. But don't let the names fool you. Power Pop is really just a polite term for punk. Well, almost. One difference between Power Pop and punk is that you don't need to wear a safety pin through your nose to like people like Elvis Costello and Nick Lowe. The emphasis now is on fun, not sheer rebellion... Elvis Costello also rejects the rock-as-art theory.

Elvis Costello - *This Year's Model*: In-depth

'That's the biggest problem with the last fifteen years of rock,' he said last year during his first US tour. 'People always claim it's art — and it's not.' But even more than Lowe, Costello's music lives up to the classic rock 'n' roll pulse. His songs and vocals bristle with a purity and conviction that is rare in the seventies. Costello's *My Aim Is True* was one of the ten best albums of 1977, and the new *This Year's Model* is even stronger. Produced by Lowe, *Model* is better designed musically. The lyrics aren't as stirring initially, but the vocals are more biting and the themes are equally potent. For the most part, they again deal with frustration and rejection, romantic and otherwise. 'Radio, Radio' is a splendid slap at the blandness of the top forty and apathy of much of today's rock audience: 'Some of my friends sit around every evening...' Except for two routine numbers, the tunes are arresting, full-bodied works that don't just sound like yet another copy of whatever sold well six months ago. 'No Action', 'Hand In Hand' and 'This Year's Girl' are vibrant, individual works. 'You Belong To Me' combines some Rolling Stones swagger with taunting Dylanish lyrics that object to romantic possessiveness. 'Pump It Up', the LP's most dynamic track, mixes dazzling lyrics with the sensual intensity of Roy Head's mid sixties 'Treat Her Right'. The encouraging thing about Costello is that he doesn't appear to be just a critic's favourite. His first album has been on the charts for five months and the new one is getting the kind of airplay that should push it into the top twenty. An American tour with Lowe this spring should boost him even further."

In the same month, *This Year's Model* was reviewed in *Billboard*; "This is a strong follow-up to last year's *My Aim Is True* debut LP from this British New Wave cult figure. All songs here possess a sparkling, dynamic quality whether it's a driving rocker or slower tempo material. Costello interprets his own wry lyrics with a raw-edged vocal style and producer Lowe cushions with fine production touches such as riveting keyboard breaks. Above all else there is a tangible energy level that pervades throughout. Best cuts — 'No Action', 'Pump It Up', You Belong To Me', 'Hand In Hand', 'Lip Service', 'Radio, Radio'. Dealers — Costello is one of the more intelligent and textured of the New Wave figures."

Some reviews made strong comparisons to Costello's debut album. Such was the case when *This Year's Model* was reviewed in

A Legacy

It's Only Rock 'N' Roll in May 1978; "When Columbia puts Costello on the label instead of its own name you know the man has arrived. Last year's model, *My Aim Is True*, became the sleeper of the year, and was most critics' choice as one of the best albums of '77. While *My Aim Is True* hit you right between the eyes, Elvis' latest doesn't have that same immediate impact. It takes a few listens to get to you, but it's just as stunning a record. Again, Nick Lowe produces but the sound is tighter on this one and the arrangements are more polished. A lot of the change has to do with Elvis working with The Attractions, the same band he toured with, instead of Clover, the pickup band on his last LP. They work well together as a unit with the organ pumping along Elvis' dangerous music. The backup vocals are much stronger here too. The lyrics to the songs remain as compelling as ever and you still have to dig for them due to Lowe's production. But that's part of the fun of Elvis' records. He always has that sound you get out of your radio, like the Stones' records. Every song on the LP has single potential, even more so than the great tunes on his last effort. Elvis is still angry and ready to take on women and the whole world with a vengeance. 'This Year's Girl' with its swirling organ lines, is delivered with a snarl and a withering gaze. It's the type of song Lennon used to write. 'No Action' has a Who-like arrangement and should especially be ear-marked for single action. 'Pump It Up' is a great dance tune written in the Chuck Berry/Dylan 'Subterranean Homesick Blues' mould. It's followed by the bluesy 'Little Triggers', a change of pace number about the agony of waiting on a phone call from a girl. 'I don't wanna be hung up, strung up, when you don't call up!' In 'Hand In Hand' on side two he tells his girl, 'If I'm gonna go down you're gonna come with me.' Elvis' women should know better than to cross him. The notorious 'Lip Service' is here and has a running motor feel to it as well as an immediacy you can't shake. 'Living In Paradise' (where 'everyone carries a gun') is as infectious as anything he's done. It sports a 'Baby Elephant Walk' organ riff then breaks into a Graham Parker-ish chorus line. The brilliantly hypnotic 'Lipstick Vogue' features great drumming by Pete Thomas and here, Lowe's production work really shines. 'Radio, Radio', Elvis' bitter salvo at the media, is here in all its glory. Elvis delivers his barbs more passionately here than on any other song. I dare anyone to play it on an AM station. It's hard for anyone to live up to

Elvis Costello - *This Year's Model*: In-depth

a first album that has become a classic, but Elvis has delivered again with *This Year's Model*. The only thing I can find fault with is the lack of Elvis' tasty guitar work, which was used only sparingly last time. The organ handles the lead lines very effectively, but I hope he plays more guitar on next year's model." Each to their own. Costello was quoted in the *Bastrop County Times* in July 1978; "Some people don't like the new album as much as the first (*My Aim Is True*), but it seems pretty empty to me to just keep repeating the formula, which is what Fleetwood Mac has done."

This Year's Model was reviewed in *Circus* in June 1978; "Elvis Costello could be the British version of Taxi Driver's Travis Bickle, except that unlike Bickle, Costello knows very well who the enemy is — at least, he does part of the time. *This Year's Model* hasn't half the misanthropic rage of Costello's first album, *My Aim Is True*, and a good deal of the rage Costello does manage is more than vaguely misogynist; his bitterness toward women is a match for the undisguised anti-female venom that plagues the Ramones. But in the end — more precisely, at the conclusion of both versions of his sophomore LP — he still hates in 1978 as well and as accurately as in 1977. *This Year's Model* doesn't provide an easy answer to the question raised by his erratic first album and static, often deliberately boring stage show. Is Costello a great rock artist or a minor eccentric? Is he a hero or just another rock critic, more well armed than the rest of us? Is he among the boldest of the punk/New Wave/ etc. performers or just the most marketable? Clearly, the best songs on *My Aim Is True* ('Less Than Zero', 'Mystery Dance', 'Welcome To The Working Week') have a power unmatched by most of the new songs. As often as not, the new LP is bailed out by the band, which mingles elements derived from the Stones, The Who and old wave punks (particularly Question Mark and The Mysterians, who contributed the organ attack which makes 'This Year's Girl' and 'The Beat' so heady). There's too much material here — in addition to the ten songs common to both versions, the US LP has one additional track, the British album two more plus a 45 — for the quality to keep up completely. And the best songs common to both albums are up to the first LP's standard: 'You Belong To Me' is a neat merger of 'The Last Time' with 'My Generation', 'Pump It Up' and 'The Beat' are exhilarating, 'Lip Service' pukes twice and shows its razor, to borrow the old Ronnie Hawkins metaphor for gut-bucket hard rock. Every one of these songs, however, is marred by Costello's sexual problems, which are severe; he must be the most carnally frustrated rock singer since Mick Jagger. Anti-female insults abound: 'Every time I phone you/I just want to put you down.' 'I don't wanna be your lover/I just wanna be your victim.' 'You wanna torture her/You wanna talk to her.' Calling this stuff unhealthy is an act of kindness or charity. Interestingly enough, at least two of the songs from which I took those lines, 'The Beat' and 'Pump It Up', are simply extended masturbation metaphors, perhaps the most ingenious since side two of *Aftermath*. Still, even this is offset by the country song on the British 45, 'Stranger In The House', which sounds to me like an allegory about identity crisis brought on by fatherhood. 'Stranger' is pure country — Elvis sounds like a single Everly Brother — and one of the best of his new songs."

The review continued; "But the very best are precisely those where he moves away from sex and romance and into other arenas. 'Night Rally' which concludes the British version, is obtuse; it may be Costello's vision of what is likely to happen to him if he continues to taunt British fascists, as he did Oswald Mosley, their leader, in 'Less Than Zero'. Or it may be his vision of everybody's multi-national future; there is a giant corporate logo flashing on and off in the sky. Strangely enough, 'Night Rally' begins with a guitar riff copped from post-rockabilly music, like Jody Reynolds' 'Endless Sleep', only the sleep Costello has in mind is more political than physical. As he says in 'Radio, Radio', 'You either shut up or get cut up.' 'Radio, Radio' is probably best known as the unrecorded song that Costello did — unrehearsed — on *Saturday Night Live* last summer, thereby pissing off the show's producer, Lorne Michaels. If Michaels had known what Costello was singing, he might have been angrier; 'Radio, Radio' is probably the most radical song anyone has recorded in the past ten years. When we think about political courage and commitment among rock stars, we generally imagine Bob Dylan's songs about black martyrs or California flyweights battling nuclear proliferation and whale-slayers. 'Radio, Radio' goes farther — Costello has put his entire career on the line by challenging the decadence and aesthetic totalitarianism of the broadcast establishment. He may get more airplay than the rest of his punkish peers combined but he's not

Elvis Costello - *This Year's Model*: In-depth

buying in and 'Radio, Radio' not only says so, it says why: 'I want to bite the hand that feeds me... make them wish they'd never seen me.' Of course, those lines are also an implicit fuck you to every record company executive and music business phony who's ever told a rock musician how much more "successful" he'd be if he'd only compromise his sound for airplay, and to every rock musician who has ever done so. As punk rock gallops off into the corporate sunset, buying into the very system it originally opposed, 'Radio, Radio' is not just an act of vengeance and wrath. It has the force of a cold blast of truth in a furnace of lies."

In all fairness, the following review by *Record Mirror* in March 1978 does hit on something in terms of some of the simplicity of the lyrics on *This Year's Model*. That is to say that there are frequently occurring phrases and patterns. Whether or not they are to the detriment of the album is probably very subjective though: "Once upon a time it wasn't that difficult to believe those (in retrospect) fatuous rumours that Elvis Costello was a figment of Nick Lowe's imagination. His voice and approach to songs were so startlingly similar to Lowe's that some sort of comparison was pretty inevitable. This no longer applies. Although Lowe produced *This Year's Model*, he has skimmed off his own ghost. Elvis is Elvis is Elvis now, and it doesn't detract one bit. This is a less whitewashed, less vicious effort than *My Aim Is True*, but the bile still spills here and there. 'I don't wanna kiss you...' lip-curls from 'No Action'. And 'I don't wanna be your lover...' from 'The Beat'. And... 'I don't wanna be hung up...' from 'Little Triggers'. I don't wanna this and I don't wanna that. The man is still an Aladdin's Cave of anti-matter, the big negative. But I don't wanna listen to the words that much, because they're not so important. What does matter is that Elvis really isn't a one album wonder, and who suspected for a moment that he was? Nick Lowe isn't the last pop craftsman; and neither is Elvis, but they're both of one breed, i.e. the short, melodic masterpiece. I find it difficult to wax eloquent about Costello, because he is a very simple artist. That isn't to suggest that he isn't personally complex — sure he's quite as twisted as he wants us to believe — but his product is like Ramones music, clever in its very lack of detail. There is some sort of formula to this album, though it isn't a strict one. The sound is very dominant keyboard and upfront bass/drum sound, with a feel not a galaxy away from the noise Blondie makes, with those same sixties-trapped ten years on atmospherics. The voice is the magic wand that transforms *This Year's Model* into something unusual, something more than pop vogue. Nasal, almost asthmatic, it somehow manages to convey a strength that belies its superficial weedyness, sort of insubstantial but wiry. Looking at it through corporation eyes, this could be construed as an attempt to conquer the American AM market, which he's already dented. *This Year's Model* is definitely more Transatlantic than *My Aim Is True*, graced with that nice fat production that the Yanks suck up so uncritically. It isn't particularly welcome — I liked that very sparse approach — but then it's hardly going to detract from songs with the qualities of '(I Don't Want To Go To) Chelsea', 'Lipstick Vogue', 'No Action' and 'The Beat'. There are a couple of unremarkable rather than puny tracks — 'You Belong To Me' and 'Pump It Up', then nobody's perfect. Elvis is getting closer though, closer all the time. God help his ego and us all if he reaches it."

This Year's Model was reviewed in the *Bangor Daily News* in April 1978; "As anyone who enjoyed *My Aim Is True* knows, Costello is not one to mince words. Now, *This Year's Model* continues where the first album left off and rest assured Elvis' success has not tempered his iconoclasm one iota. Of the eleven songs, only 'Radio, Radio' is targeted at an institution; the other ten (particularly 'No Action', 'Hand In Hand' and 'Lip Service') are directed at individuals who have rejected the singer in some way. For Costello, the rejection is rechannelled into resentment, revenge and spite — at times chillingly so. Costello leers about 'changing someone's facial design.' Yet, Costello's rather narrow-minded themes are guised as wondrously tight rock 'n' roll — upbeat, punchy keyboard frills, driving bass lines and propulsive tom toms keep the songs charging ahead, each unique in itself. Costello himself plays sparse guitar, entirely rhythmic, and reserves the spare instrumental breaks for the others. Vocally, he is reminiscent of Springsteen, but the comparisons end at that point. Springsteen envelopes his scenarios with embellished characters and a variety of contrasting themes and images. Costello will have none of it; his songs are manically urgent, and to the point, as if he's eager to get on with it and attack another subject. Still, for all his speed, Costello is careful with phrasings; words placed in and around the beat and melody work expertly. This juxtaposition of vibrant rock

Elvis Costello - *This Year's Model*: In-depth

(with influences as varied as the pub scene and reggae) and taut expressive vocals make *This Year's Model* a success on par with *My Aim Is True*. Costello may, in the future, have to expand his concerns beyond his current preoccupations, but he is now an inventive and creative artist who will achieve an even wider audience with this album. Look for heavy FM airplay."

Creem reviewed *This Year's Model* in July 1978; "Isn't that always the greatest affront to the sleuth, when the focal clue has to practically chew up his 99-cent support stockings for him to notice it? So comes my chagrin upon finally solving this album's enigma: Elvis Costello sings through a camera. Cut and dry, the evidence right there on the record jacket. Guy just isolates himself in some snot-coloured cubicle and sings into a camera; 'grrr.' The effect is like Graham Parker and Blondie albums lain one atop the other on the summer sidewalks of NYC, trod upon and melted into a hybrid. Or maybe ultimately like what the world would have to deal with were Graham to seduce Blondie, or more likely vice-versa, upon a bed of insulated electrical wires which, post-consummation of the act, were fused inextricably to the abdomen of the lust-child-infested mother, and with first breath, the bastard whispers, 'radio, radio...' It is obvious that Costello's only fear is that his fearless music will go unheard. That he should be at all equated with punk is merely a two-fold misfortune; part temporal, and the main part due to his aggressive stance — a first-sensed difference from at least the initial British New Wave manifesto is that Elvis' motif is less politicultural than interpersonal, and especially contemptuous of the fairer sex (or unfairer sex, as he would have it). Now while he doesn't piece in with that contingent, he does nonetheless prove quite stylistically mindful; distinct enough from any other extant act to be noted, yet cautious of excess experimentation in this establishmental sophomore phase. I must confess that a lyric outlay would have helped me in several places, what with Elvis either pinching his voice, as if priming a retrievable poison dart, or rushing speedword exhalings through those doubtlessly gritted choppers of his. And chop they do; with *My Aim Is True*, almost all the songs here are centrally and virulently concerned with women — piqued by them, pricked by them, loathing and longing them, or belittling the musclemass studs that possess them, while he's left out in the cold. Now, while I don't happen to identify with his particular view of things, this alone doesn't prove reason enough for me to dislike the record — the arrangements are so just right methodically odd (quirkrock?) that I've found myself singing lyrics which, under saner circumstances, I wouldn't subscribe to. I don't know, sometimes this revelation comes to me — I foresee some klan-destine thing involved in this new world recordry; a sort of anti-snatch rape-rooter's beat-that-butch-Doberman-bitch-'til-she-suffers kinda thing, so tell me, are your best girl's eyes looking suddenly blackenable?"

This Year's Model was reviewed in *Village Voice* in April 1978; "This is not punk rock. But anyone who thinks it's uninfluenced should compare the bite and drive of the backup here to the well-played studio pub-rock of his debut and ask themselves how come he now sounds as angry as he says he feels. I find his snarl more compelling musically and verbally than all his melodic and lyrical tricks, and while I still wish he liked girls more, at least I'm ready to believe he's had some bad luck."

And in the *Canberra Times* in July 1978; "Elvis Costello is, in my books, one of the best of the New Wave artists to emerge from the UK. And about time some class makes it onto the charts, good honest music. His songs have found their place in US and Australian charts. When I first saw a photo of Elvis Costello early last year, I thought, who is this zany character, is he trying to cash in on Presley, or what? A sour impression indeed, but it wasn't till I heard his music, played constantly by Maree, an avid Costello fan, on 2XX, that I was unavoidably attracted and stimulated by this romantic rock 'n' roller."

This Year's Model was reviewed in *Crawdaddy* in June 1978; "Somebody must have told Elvis Costello about "the Mystery Dance" — sex. All about it. Told him, showed him — and burned him so badly that the idea of romance scares the living hell out of him, yet he can't get sex off his mind. On all but one song ('Radio, Radio', which doesn't appear on the British version), *This Year's Model* stays close to the thick of sexual warfare. Elvis vs. fear and lies, Elvis vs. anyone who gets close. Presumably, this album is not an autobiography of Declan Patrick MacManus, happily married father of one, but of his stage persona 'Elvis Costello'. I just wonder where he gets so much venom. *This Year's Model* shows none of the

Elvis Costello - *This Year's Model*: In-depth

detachment of *My Aim Is True*. The band (Costello's own Attractions instead of the San Francisco band Clover) plays much harder, and the lyrics stay personal. No politics, very little philosophy (although 'Night Rally' on the British version has a bit of both). Costello is still bugged by the same thing: 'Knowing you're with him is driving me crazy' ('No Action'). This time, though, he won't 'try to be amused' at rejection or infidelity. He cultivates his rage, to flash it at strangers, indiscriminately. Betrayed over and over again in the songs, Costello can barely contain himself. Desire, fear, anger and guilt merge in these songs, and the mixture is volatile. Elvis equates lust with crime ('The Beat') and terrorism ('Lip Service'); he shouldn't be surprised when his partners turn out to be duplicitous ('Living In Paradise'). No matter how many times Elvis sings 'I don't wanna' on this LP, he can't escape his longing. 'Sometimes I think that love is just a tumour,' Costello blurts in 'Lipstick Vogue', but he has to 'get to the slot machine' and 'insert the token' anyway. His denials define his need. Even on the album's attempt at fairness, 'This Year's Girl' — about a Farrah-type cover girl icon — Costello can't hold back lines like 'You want her broken with her mouth wide open'."

The review continued; "Although the rhythm track for 'This Year's Girl' takes after Donovan's 'Sunshine Superman' there's no way it, or any other song on *This Year's Model*, could sound as genial, superficially, as 'Alison' or 'Waiting For The End Of The World'. Costello is almost continuously savage. The LP's sole ballad, a standard 12/8 soul progression called 'Little Triggers', snarls unmistakably, and when its chorus of Elvises sings 'ooh,' they sound like leashed, hungry Dobermans, not the Jordanaires. Mellow-sound airplay won't be forthcoming. Hence 'Radio, Radio', a Springsteen/Spectorised blast at programmers 'trying to anesthetise the way that you feel.' (This media paranoia serves as a respite of sorts from Elvis' consistent misogyny). Costello and The Attractions play midsixties dance music with afterburners blazing. Drums and guitar for weight and thrust, cheesy organ for manoeuvring. 'Pump It Up', a petrol-pusher's ode to masturbation, thumps like a subterranean homesick Stax track, and 'Lip Service' is semi-gloss Searchers/Lovin' Spoonful pop. 'The Beat''s verses resemble Bacharach/David tunes, while 'Living In Paradise' approaches reggae. Under Nick Lowe's production, Costello avoids New Wave monotony; these arrangements ambush you with carefully plotted dynamics. Lowe's tricks (the handclaps in 'Lip Service', a fusillade of drums in 'The Beat', multiple vocal overdubs on 'No Action') are perfectly placed, although he does permit some utterly inept tambourine playing on 'Hand In Hand.' Costello has outgrown his Dylan worship; he sings in his own voice now. But his melodic gift is limited — he uses variations on the common descending scale so often that the exceptions ('Hand In Hand' and 'No Action') seem catchy by contrast — so Lowe has to sneak in some instrumental hooks, too. No doubt about it — *This Year's Model* rocks tough and committed. It is also so wrongheaded, so full of hatred, and so convinced of its moral superiority that it makes me uneasy. Costello's intelligence is evident in every lyric; it's easy to identify, for a little while, with his pained vindictiveness. I learned about love from pop songs, though, and these 'don't tell me anything about it I don't know already.' Costello distrusts his entire universe, particularly its female side, and I get the feeling negativity won't pull him through."

From *Beat Instrumental* in May 1978; "The snarler is back, sounding as tortured and twisted as he did on *My Aim Is True*, but this time with his own band, The Attractions, instead of Clover, who backed his first album. The almost hysterical reaction which greeted the latter on its release was a sign of how musically desolate those times were. The press were betting on bands like they were on horses — Pistols, Damned, Clash, Buzzcocks — they all flashed past with no more than a handful of chords between them and not a single melody. As heroes they were pretty one-dimensional, but then along came Elvis with all the right hip credentials *plus* the ability to write good songs and suddenly everyone was rushing to stake their bankroll. So has he survived musically in the interval between then and now? Well, probably, but there are signs on *This Year's Model* that Elvis is having to draw on a couple of rather obvious influences — Dylan's 'Subterranean Homesick Blues' and the Stones' 'The Last Time' crop up rather alarmingly. He cocks a snook at Cliff Richard in one song with a clever pastiche of 'Summer Holiday', but though this raises a smile the first couple of times, it later becomes irritating. On the last track — 'Night Rally' — the opening riff is direct from 'And Then I Kissed Her'. None of this is really necessary because Elvis has already proved that he can write his own perfectly good hook lines.

Elvis Costello - *This Year's Model*: In-depth

'Night Rally' doesn't *depend* on that well-worn riff — so why use it? Another bitch — both arrangement and production are a little down on last time. That horrible, reedy plastic organ sound really ought to be put out to grass. It would be okay on some songs, but on others it is inappropriate. The whole album has a woolly feel to it at the bass end. What it could have used to advantage was a shade more rhythm guitar/organ, that middle area which the keyboard player so sadly neglects. The first album had everything covered in this department and was hence easier on the ear. On the credit side, there is some very fiery playing on 'Lipstick Vogue' and 'Lip Service', both of which do have the full sound that the others seem to lack, in addition to being good tunes. 'Little Triggers' is a slow song in 3/4 which allows Elvis to show that he can put something more subtle in his voice than the usual mixture of anger and jealousy. There's nothing on this album as good as 'Watching The Detectives', but like all of his songs, these take quite a lot of getting used to. It's worth giving them a chance before making any final decision, so borrow a friend's copy first!"

This Year's Model was reviewed generously in *New Musical Express* in March 1978; "There's only one real problem facing the reviewer assessing this, our El's second album, but if it's tricky enough to deal with then at least it's easy enough to define. *This Year's Model*, you see, is simply so ridiculously good that one's immediate inclinations are to clamber effusively over the top, superlative peaking superlative to the point where well-meaning enthusiasm turns an unattractive tint of bloated sycophancy. I was so awed at this record at one point that I was ready to blunder into that hoariest of clichés — the "brazen young troubadour as new Bob Dylan" line that has ended up blighting more than one or two young chappies' credibility count under a hailstorm of hyperbole. Then again, the case history of Elvis Costello does tend to throw all, uh, "orthodox perspective" out of the window. It can't be much more than a year since Costello modestly announced his talents via the 'Less Than Zero' single on Stiff. The record was potent enough to cause initial minor-league cult interest although Costello's photogenic incongruities plus the presence of arch vinyl-jesters Nick Lowe and Jake Riviera caused most spectators to chuckle, as they acknowledged Costello as little more than another Stiff crazy gang product — talented, sure, but a touch heavy on the old Graham Parker, Van Morrison, etc. influences. But then came the

A Legacy

album, *My Aim Is True*, and then things began to happen. *Aim* stood out, even in the generally incendiary context of rock's newfound action. Costello was no longer just some quirky Lowe invention but a veritable walking time bomb, a man possessed and loaded with truly dangerous visions. With *Aim* Costello established himself instantly as rock's most subversively obsessive artist of this decade. His "Sex" songs, for example, totally up-ended all the beef-cake posturings of the medium's macho patent by instead honing in with brutal self-effacement on his chosen role as sexual incompetent, all trembling flesh, guilt-ridden, and down so far he couldn't even lick his wounds. And when it came to "Love" Costello outdid even the perverse naked truth slant of the aforementioned genre by mating, in 'Alison' at least, an exquisitely tender melody with a portrait of passion turned so ugly and desperate that the singer could only osmose a mixture of disgust and despair, both harrowing and heart wrenching, at the consequences."

The review continued; "Anyway, *My Aim Is True* scored a spectacular victory last year, not merely as a critics' fave but also managing to shift a considerable weight of units both here and in the States (where even now it languishes in the lower forties). It's often savage extremities of subject matter and attitude of framed around a needle-sharp sensibility for strong musical backdrops, whether it was the raging rock swagger of 'Mystery Dance' or the irrepressible riff of 'Miracle Man', straight through to Costello's oh-so-very-deft adoption of various prime mid-sixties pop stylisations. *Aim* hit you on so many levels that even if you happened to be repelled by the more extreme aspects (and I've met many — women, most often, as it happens — who find Costello's revenge/guilt fetish persona totally unappealing), you couldn't help but be impressed by some other area of the man's astonishing talents. *Aim* hit the jackpot anyway — even finding itself cloistered in the hallowed precinct of rock's reactionary media bastion, Rolling Stones' five classic albums of '77, residing between the platinum pabulum of *Hotel California* and *Rumours* no less. And here's *This Year's Model*. A joyous event, this, a follow-up to a first-off classic that totally outstrips its predecessor (The Band's following *Big Pink* with their magnificent second album was another, albeit random, instance) in virtually every respect. Costello himself is stronger, more abrasively confident in his vocal delivery, while his songs are almost all proverbial blitzers. However, arguably the decisive improvement is the change in back-up personnel. For *Aim* Elvis was supported by West Coast exiles Clover who, though involved in a mere session-playing capacity, nonetheless consistently outdid themselves, providing some superbly emphatic playing. By the time the album had been released Costello had drawn together his own band, The Attractions, a corporate with their own sound and personality that gave a thrilling taster for things to come."

Still from the same review; "The Attractions, see, provided a tension for songs like 'Waiting For The End Of The World' that gave the song's sentiments a gripping snap that the recorded version barely hinted at, while the newer pieces were imbued with such a shuddering intensity that the ensemble seemed at times to be working on some eerie level of telepathic interaction. In this month's *Playboy* interview (easily his most revealing dialogue for over ten years) Bob Dylan described the sound he was aiming for during his cataclysmic mid-sixties electric period. He stated that 'the closest I ever got to the sound I hear in my mind was in the individual bands on the *Blonde On Blonde* album. It's metallic and bright gold, with whatever that conjures up.' What that "conjures up", in effect, is exactly the sound that Costello and The Attractions have consistently attained throughout the songs on *This Year's Model*. "That wild mercury sound" is the perfect description for the powerdrive rush through the album's most immediately stunning achievements — the already much-lauded 'Chelsea' and side two's 'Lipstick Vogue'. The latter has long been a personal fave ever since I first heard it played live, and the album version eclipses even the manic imperiousness of the stage song. Firing off at a truly fearsome intensity, Costello and band interlock as taut as a clenched fist getting tighter and tighter until the veins bulge out like railroad tracks. Costello spits out some of his most vitriolic lines: 'Don't say you love me when it's just a rumour…' Meanwhile three tracks earlier the band have staged a similarly awesome assault on the senses with 'Chelsea', a great, great single up there with 'Positively 4th Street' and 'Substitute'. *Model* is, by the way, similar to *Aim* in that it's instantly devastating moments tend to overshadow the rest. For at least a day I was transfixed between 'Lipstick' and 'Chelsea', only occasionally venturing elsewhere. Don't be fooled though — after a week spent with the record, its overall omnipotence is undeniable."

Continued: "Fave tracks constantly change until virtually all twelve numbers rank level. Next, for example, it was 'This Year's Girl' with its Beatles cop intro, hammerhead drumming and rock steady melody supporting El's sly observations on all the Farrah Fawcett-Majors of this world: 'A bright spark might...' Then came 'Living In Paradise' with its contagious limbo shuffle jerking seductively into a raging power-pop (not the trendy cliché but the real thing this time, hepcats) chorus with Costello dissecting the sick veneer of Los Angeles luxury, playing with the corporation boss, nudging with a perverse cuckold twist in 'Later in the evening when the arrangements are made...' And there's 'Little Triggers', the album's ballad and placed, strategically perhaps, at the same juncture as 'Alison' on *Aim*. At first the song disappoints — a Solomon Burke type soul thing with quirky, trembling flesh imagery. Later one uncovers a gorgeously understated melody with moments that nod towards the influence of Burt Bacharach, whose 'I Just Don't Know What To Do With Myself' Costello performed exquisitely on the *Live Stiffs* album. 'Pump It Up' is steamy and sensual with a Dylanesque raunch quotient. Like 'You Belong To Me', it is a hot-blooded example of rhythm and blues stylisation, though both songs tend to impress considerably less within the so virulently fraught confines of the album. Finally, straight after 'Lipstick', Costello chooses to exit with the grim portents of 'Night Rally'. Just as *Aim*'s finale 'Waiting For The End Of The World' portrayed a doomy and all too realistically ominous scene of social breakdown/apocalypse, so *Model* leaves the listener unnerved by an all too frighteningly vivid image of the National Front gaining influence. 'Everybody's wringing their hands...' No bloated pontificating here, no 'Eve Of Destruction' hysteria — Costello simply sees all the signs, strings them together and rounds off a chilling scene with 'You think they're so dumb...' The title phrase repeats itself over and over whilst the organ motif rings out like a siren, leaving one disoriented if not a little scared. So that's *This Year's Model* for you. Nothing's really changed, Costello's bitterness and obsessive vitriol is still there but, like Pete Townshend and Dylan before him, Costello knows that the true essence of rock as potent music is as a vehicle for frustration. Costello is currently the best. There's simply no-one within spitting

Elvis Costello - *This Year's Model*: In-depth

distance of him. He has his finger on the pulse of this desperate era and his perceptions are so disquieting because all too often they're too damn real to be strenuously ignored. Meanwhile *Model* is just too powerful, too dazzling to be ignored or sidestepped. Uneasy listening. The perfect antidote to the placebo syndrome. Recoil at your peril."

The success of *This Year's Model* was very much down to a team effort. The Attractions proved to be Costello's most well-known musical associates. The album marked the beginning of working relationship that would span nine more studio albums up to and including *Blood & Chocolate* in 1986. There was also a reunion for *All This Useless Beauty* released in 1996. One of the most impressive things about *This Year's Model*, perhaps, is the fact that the attitude that comes across was not to the determinant of the musicality overall; anger and bitterness was portrayed without the need for roaring vocals and distorted riffing, as was the case with many other bands in the punk and New Wave vein at the time. Whilst it wouldn't be fair to try and elevate the status of *This Year's Model* above other major punk and New Wave albums of the late seventies, it seems reasonable to say that the album brought something slightly different to the table that placed more emphasis on melody than just on anger.

By August 1978, Costello and The Attractions were already beginning to work on Costello's third album at Eden Studios. It was given the provisional title of *Emotional Fascism*. The album wasn't finished before it was time for them to go to the Far East and Australia to tour. Meanwhile, 'Radio, Radio' was released as a single in the UK where it fell just shy of a top twenty position. A new song from the August 1978 sessions was put on the B-side of the single. Titled 'Tiny Steps', it wasn't to be included on the album that came to be called *Armed Forces*.

The latter was released in January 1979. It was Costello's first and only top ten album in the US (understandable really considering the impact that he and The Attractions had made whilst touring after the release of *This Year's Model*). The single, 'Oliver's Army', got to number two in the UK.

Also, 'Accidents Will Happen' got into the top thirty. *Armed Forces* itself got to number two in the UK. It also had success in Canada where it got to number eight and in Australia where it got to number nine. 'Senior Service' was given generous airplay in Australia. It was after adding 'What's So Funny ('Bout Peace Love And Understanding)' to the US version of *Armed Forces* that Columbia Records decided to release 'Accidents Will Happen' as a single. It fell just short of the top one hundred though (it was just on the cusp at number one hundred and one!).

Even though 'Oliver's Army' did well outside of the US, Columbia were reluctant to release it as a single there due to the "white nigger" reference that occurs in the second verse.

Armed Forces was reviewed in *Melody Maker* in December; "The Mystery Dance for 1979 sounds like a step sideways. *Armed Forces* consolidates everything that Elvis Costello achieved with The Attractions on *This Year's Model*. Some of the songs and arrangements here would have fitted on the previous album; others seem designed to "stretch" the band and demonstrate its flexibility. There's less gut attack, less overall aggression this time; instead a more relaxed display of energy and precision, of the kind that springs from unusual self-confidence. And the confidence is largely justified. Who else currently makes twelve-cut albums without a single duff track? But it's still a sideways step. Costello has moved away from the put-down-by-numbers approach of his earlier songwriting towards — what? A "concept"? The elaborate album package loudly announces one, maybe even two or three. Take the title, which connects with some of the graphics on the awkward wrap-around sleeve, and with references to militarism in several of the songs. It might also connect with the instruction 'Don't Join', printed on The Attractions postcards that are flimsily attached to the sleeve; perhaps Elvis is telling us not to sign up in the services. Then there's the cover painting of elephants, which doesn't seem to have anything much to do with the lyrics but doubtless relates to the leopard spots and zebra stripes that infest the album label. Not to mention the obligatory fake-surrealism of the inner sleeve, or the fairly grim collage of modern art styles (from hard-edge abstraction through abstract expressionism to op and pop) that garnishes the inside of the main sleeve. Recent years have given everyone plenty of practice in ignoring overkill packaging and concentrating on the actual music, but in this case the conflicting implications of the (unsigned) artwork raise provocative questions about the songs inside. Neither

Elvis Costello - *This Year's Model*: In-depth

the artwork nor the songs would stand as what the Surrealists called "actes gratuites", things in and of themselves: both are riddled with far too many outside references for that and yet any attempt to square them off with the things they refer to flounders on their obliqueness or outright obscurity. The album opens with Costello singing that he just doesn't know where to begin as the preface to what sounds like a retraction of some sort: 'You used to be a victim...' The song is 'Accidents Will Happen', also featured on the live EP that comes free with the package, in a simpler and more moving version. And it closes with another autobiographical "statement": 'Two little Hitlers will fight it out until...'. I have no idea what those lines might mean to their author, but if they have a "public" meaning it must be that he is trying to transcend the motifs of recrimination and vindictiveness that have certainly dominated his work thus far."

The review continued; "Sure enough, most of the other songs here either use a fictionalised "I" or look outwards at society or the world at large. It's a refreshing turn and it would be even more refreshing if Costello grasped the courage of his convictions and came out with a coherent point of view. There's no rule that says a rock song has to be "about" something, but if you start singing about being 'in Palestine/ Overrun by the Chinese line' then your consumers have a right to start asking questions. To take one example, 'Sunday's Best' uses a naggingly jaunty calliope-style backing for some quite credible English social commentary in the Ray Davies tradition until the lyric gets lost in melodrama about severed heads under the bed. It then hits the verse: 'Listen to the decent people...' What does that mean? Does it refer back to conscription? (There are some bizarre time transitions elsewhere, as when Costello refers to walking in polka dots and chequered slacks). Or is it supposed to invoke some threatening future? Either way, it's at best feeble and at worst offensive. Similarly, 'Oliver's Army' is just fine when it starts out as the reverie of someone dreaming of a career in the army, but it becomes specious when the regular army blurs into a mercenary force, and it seems to me to lose all credibility when it refers to Hong Kong being up for grabs in one breath and to Mr Churchill in the next. Political acumen that's not, and neither does it offer an interesting historical perspective. I wish I could make more sense of it; I've tried and I've tried, and I'm still mystified. If there is a governing "concept", it's probably the one signalled on the inner sleeve: 'emotional fascism'. It's a theme that Costello alternately evades and indulges, and the most promising thing about the album is undoubtedly the hint that he's beginning to get it into perspective. But his lyrics are still happiest when they move through genuinely random-sounding free-associations, at their best equal to anything by Eno. There are many highly memorable formulations in the wordplay: 'I'm in a grip-like vice' ('Party Girl'), 'It's the death that's worse than fate' ('Senior Service'), 'There's a shorthand typist taking seconds over minutes' ('Green Shirt'). And anyway, the music is strong enough to swamp virtually any lapses in the lyrics — literally so in 'Goon Squad', whose words elude repeated hearings, and metaphorically so throughout. Costello's tunes are rarely original but invariably fresh, and even the outright lifts (like the Beatles' fade that ends side one) have a grace worthy of producer Nick Lowe. Steve Nieve's keyboards, in particular, have a range and bite that is unique in contemporary rock; it falls to him to introduce most of the gorgeous cross-melodies that distinguish many of the songs, and he brings it off every time with terrific finesse. What's more, Costello's vocal phrasing is getting richer all the time (as is his stage presence, judging by last week's showings at The Dominion in London): listen to his handling of the rhythm of the long chorus line in 'Moods For Moderns', or the expert mixture of bombast, sarcasm and quiet menace in 'Big Boys'. Hell, whichever way it's moving, it's more excellent than not. Enough writing; I'm going to listen to it again. I can't do it any more, and I'm not satisfied."

By the time it was released, *Armed Forces* had been a relatively long time in the making considering everything that had happened since work began on it. When asked what direction he expected his third album to go in, Costello was quoted in *New Musical Express* in March 1978; "A progression — I want to plough in more emotions, not because people have drawn this one-dimensional picture of me but just for my own sanity, really."

When asked if he already had some songs planned, he was quoted in the same feature; "Oh, about fifteen. There's 'Sunday's Best', which is nothing more than a commentary on the English way of life, as far as I can see. There's 'Dr Luther's Assistant' which I mentioned before, where Luther is this Howard Hughes sort of figure and his assistant, well, you'll hear it soon enough. There's another

Elvis Costello - *This Year's Model*: In-depth

one called 'Chemistry Class' which I do solo and also 'Green Shirt' which is an offshoot of 'The Beat' in a way. These songs will be more, uh, outward looking. Like, there's less humour on *Model* than the last, don't you think? It's more vicious overall but far less personal, though. But then my sense of humour is very, very bleak, very low key... I don't think I'm obsessed with one idea. In fact I know I'm not, or else I would be completely happy to play up to the image of me as a one-dimensional revengeful character all the time."

Rolling Stone placed *This Year's Model* at number eleven in a list of best albums from 1967 to 1987. Not only that, but Costello's first three albums were all included on *Rolling Stone*'s Five Hundred Greatest Albums Of All Time list.

Since splitting from The Attractions in 1986, the majority of Costello's work has been as a solo artist. As is the case on *This Year's Model*, his lyrics still continue to contain an exponential vocabulary teamed with frequent wordplay. The way in which his music has drawn on a range of genres over the years is demonstrative that he is able to reinvent music from the past in a way that makes it his own. It could be said that this has always been the case; *This Year's Model* embraces strong moments of not only rock, but reggae. Throughout his fruitful career, Costello would go on to cover a range of genres including jazz, country and opera.

It is amazing to think that despite the distinctive style present in *This Year's Model*, Costello's second album would be just the beginning in terms of broader exploration. Costello has co-writing credits on numerous film songs. They include 'God Give Me Strength' written with Burt Bacharach for the 1996 film, *Grace Of My Heart* and 'The Scarlet Tide' written with T-Bone Burnett for the 2003 film, *Cold Mountain*.

For the latter, Costello and Burnett were nominated for a Grammy Award for Best Song Written For Visual Media as well as for an Academy Award for Best Original Song. Costello was inducted into the Rock and Roll Hall of Fame in 2003.

A year later, he was listed by *Rolling Stone* at number eighty in a list by the title of, The One Hundred Greatest Artists Of All Time.

Costello has worked as a producer for Squeeze, The Pogues, Madness, and The Specials. He was asked by former Transmission Vamp singer, Wendy James, if he would write a song for her to use on her 1993 debut solo album, *Now Ain't The Time For Your Tears*. Not only did he write one song, he wrote a whole album's worth! In just one afternoon! Considering the speed at which *This Year's Model* was made, this fact probably isn't too surprising but still, it adds weight to just how prolific Costello has remained over the years since.

So how does *This Year's Model* hold up today? Well, it does sound very much of its time but the ideas and innovation — and indeed energy — still have a freshness to them that make it a classic album. It documents a pivotal achievement in Elvis Costello's career — in and of itself and in terms of marking the start of a long-term working relationship with The Attractions. Equally, it packages a range of social commentary and in-yer-face observations and emotions into something that is pleasurably melodic within accessible song structures. Overall, a strong album with a lasting legacy and plenty of replay value.

Elvis Costello - *This Year's Model*: In-depth

This Year's Model
A Comprehensive Discography

Personnel

Elvis Costello — guitar, vocals

The Attractions:
Steve Nieve — piano, organ
Bruce Thomas — bass
Pete Thomas — drums
with:
Mick Jones — lead guitar on Big Tears
Nick Lowe - producer

Track Listing

All songs written by Elvis Costello

Side One
1. No Action (1:58)
2. This Year's Girl (3:17)
3. The Beat (3:45)
4. Pump It Up (3:14)
5. Little Triggers (2:40)
6. You Belong To Me (2:22)

Side Two
1. Hand In Hand (2:33)
2. (I Don't Want To Go To) Chelsea (3:07)
3. Lip Service (2:36)
4. Living In Paradise (3:52)
5. Lipstick Vogue (3:42)
6. Night Rally (2:41)

The US release on Columbia, two months after the original UK release, dropped '(I Don't Want To Go To) Chelsea' and 'Night Rally' and added 'Radio, Radio' to close side two.

Bonus Tracks (1993 Rykodisc CD)

13. Radio, Radio (3:05)
14. Big Tears (3:09)
15. Crawling In The USA (2:53)
16. Running Out Of Angels (demo) (2:02)
17. Green Shirt (demo) (2:20)
18. Big Boys (demo) (3:00)

Bonus Disc (2002 Rhino CD)

Big Tears (3:12)
Crawling To The USA (2:55)
Running Out Of Angels (demo) (2:05)
Green Shirt (demo) (2:22)
Big Boys (demo) (3:00)
You Belong To Me (Capital Radio version) (1:55)
Radio, Radio (Capital Radio version) (3:01)
Neat Neat Neat (Brian James) (live) (3:16)
Roadette Song (Ian Dury, Russell Hardy) (live) (5:40)
This Year's Girl (Alternate Eden Studios version) (2:09)
(I Don't Want To Go To) Chelsea (Basing Street Studios version) (3:00)
Stranger In The House (BBC version) (4:15)

While the Rykodisc version contains the original album and bonus tracks on one CD, the Rhino version has two CDs. Disc one contains the original UK album plus Radio, Radio and disc two contains bonus tracks.

Deluxe edition (2008 Hip-O/Universal CD)

Disc One
No Action (2:01)
This Year's Girl (3:22)
The Beat (3:48)
Pump It Up (3:17)
Little Triggers (2:43)
You Belong to Me (2:25)
Hand In Hand (2:38)
(I Don't Want To Go To) Chelsea (3:10)
Lip Service (2:39)
Living In Paradise (3:47)
Lipstick Vogue (3:33)
Night Rally — 2:46
Radio, Radio (3:12)
Big Tears (3:12)

Crawling To The USA (2:54)
Tiny Steps (2:44)
Running Out Of Angels (demo) (2:04)
Green Shirt (demo) (2:22)
Big Boys (demo) (3:00)
Neat Neat Neat (live) (3:16)
Roadette Song (live) (5:40)
This Year's Girl (Alternate Eden Studios version) (2:09)
(I Don't Want To Go To) Chelsea (Alternate Basing Street Studios version) (2:57)

Disc Two (Live at the Warner Theatre, Washington, DC, 28th February 1978)
Pump It Up (3:31)
Waiting For The End Of The World (3:59)
No Action (2:28)
Less Than Zero (4:29)
The Beat (3:43)
(The Angels Wanna Wear My) Red Shoes (2:35)
(I Don't Want To Go To) Chelsea (3:58)
Hand In Hand (2:53)
Little Triggers (3:08)
Radio, Radio (2:37)
You Belong To Me (2:54)
Lipstick Vogue (5:02)
Watching The Detectives (6:02)
Mystery Dance (3:58)
Miracle Man (4:25)
Blame It On Cain (4:05)
Chemistry Class (solo acoustic) (2:44)

Chemistry Class is a solo acoustic recording which was previously released on the 2002 Rhino re-issue of *Armed Forces*

Original UK release, 17th March 1978:
Radar RAD 3, LP
Radar RAC 3, cassette

Reissues:
F-Beat XXLP4, LP, 1980
Imp Records, FIEND 18, LP, 1984
Imp Records IMP FIEND CASS 18, cassette, 1984
Imp Records IMP FIEND CD 18, CD,1986
Demon Records DPAM 2, CD, 1993
Edsel Records MANUS 102, CD, 2002

Original US releases, March 1978:
Columbia JC 35331, LP

Columbia PCT 35331, cassette
Columbia JCA 35331, 8-track

Reissues:
Columbia PC 35331, LP, 1984
Columbia CK 35331, CD, 1986
Rykodisc RCD 10272, CD, 1993
Rhino Records R2 78354, CD, 2002
Hip-O Records B0008638-02, CD, 2007
Hip-O Records B0010681-02, CD, 2008
Mobile Fidelity Sound Lab MFSL 1-330, LP, 2010

SINGLES

UK

(I Don't Want To Go To) Chelsea / You Belong To Me
Radar Records ADA 3, 3rd March 1978

Pump It Up / Big Tears
Radar Records ADA 10, 28th April 1978

Radio Radio / Tiny Steps
Radar Records ADA 24, 20th October 1978

USA

This Year's Girl / Big Tears
Columbia 3-10762, May 1978

Tour Dates

1977

Friday 27th May	Nashville Rooms, London
Saturday 28th May	Nashville Rooms, London
Thursday 14th July	The Garden, Penzance, England
Friday 15th July	Woods Centre, Plymouth, England
Saturday 16th July	Village Hall, Davidstow, England
Thursday 21st July	Rafters, Manchester, England,
Tuesday 26th July	Hilton Hotel, London, England

Impromptu performance in front of the hotel during the CBS press conference.

Tuesday 26th July	Dingwalls, London, England
Wednesday 27th July	Hope And Anchor, London, England
Thursday 28th July	Nags Head, High Wycombe, England
Friday 29th July	Polytechnic, Huddersfield, England
Tuesday 2nd August	Eric's, Liverpool, England
Sunday 7th August	Nashville Rooms, London, England
Thursday 11th August	Jazz Bilzen, Bilzen, Belgium
Saturday 13th August	Hope And Anchor, London, England
Sunday 14th August	Nashville Rooms, London, England
Monday 15th August	The Affair, Swindon, England
Saturday 20th August	Popfestival, Marseille, France
Sunday 21st August	Nashville Rooms, London, England
Monday 22nd August	Castaways, Plymouth, England
Friday 26th August	The Penthouse, Scarborough, England
Saturday 27th August	JB's Club, Dudley, England
Sunday 28th August	Nashville Rooms, London, England
Tuesday 30th August	Silver Thread Hotel, Paisley, Scotland
Wednesday 31st August	Tiffany's, Edinburgh, Scotland
Thursday 1st September	Maniqui, Falkirk, Scotland
Sunday 4th September	Nashville Rooms, London, England
Saturday 10th September	Garden Party X, Crystal Palace Bowl, London, England
Monday 3rd October	Town Hall, High Wycombe, England
Tuesday 4th October	University, Aberystwyth, Wales
Thursday 6th October	Exhibition Centre, Bristol, England
Friday 7th October	University, Bath, England
Saturday 8th October	University, Loughborough, England
Sunday 9th October	Town Hall, Middlesbrough, England
Tuesday 11th October	Empire Theatre, Liverpool, England
Thursday 13th October	Apollo Theatre, Glasgow, Scotland
Friday 14th October	Polytechnic, Sheffield, England
Saturday 15th October	University, Leeds, England
Sunday 16th October	Fairfield Hall Croydon, England
Tuesday 18th October	University Of East Anglia, Norwich, England
Wednesday 19th October	Top Rank Suite, Brighton, England
Friday 21st October	Apollo Theatre, Manchester, England
Saturday 22nd October	University of Leicester, Leicester, England
Monday 24th October	Champness Hall, Rochdale, England
Tuesday 25th October	Town Hall, Birmingham, England
Wednesday 26th October	Top Rank Suite, Cardiff, England
Thursday 27th October	Civic Hall, Wolverhampton, England
Friday 28th October	Lyceum Ballroom, London, England
Monday 31st October	Civic Hall, Guildford, England
Wednesday 2nd November	Friars At The Vale Hall, Aylesbury, England
Thursday 3rd November	University of Essex, Colchester, England
Friday 4th November	Polytechnic, Newcastle upon Tyne, England
Saturday 5th November	Lancaster University, Lancaster, England
Tuesday 15th November	Old Waldorf, San Francisco, CA, USA *(matinee & evening shows)*

Wednesday 16th November	Old Waldorf, San Francisco, CA, USA *(matinee & evening shows)*
Friday 18th November	Whisky a Go Go, Los Angeles, CA, USA
Saturday 19th November	Whisky a Go Go, Los Angeles, CA, USA
Wednesday 23rd November	Jed's, New Orleans, LA, USA
Saturday 26th November	Capri Theatre, Atlanta, GA, USA
Sunday 27th November	American Theatre, St. Louis, MO, USA
Tuesday 29th November	Bunky's, Madison, WI, USA
Wednesday 30th November	B'Ginnings, Schaumburg, IL, USA
Thursday 1st December	Electric Ballroom, Milwaukee, WI, USA
Friday 2nd December	Riviera Theatre, Chicago, IL, USA
Monday 5th December	Agora Ballroom, Cleveland, OH, USA
Tuesday 6th December	Four Acres Club, Marcy, NY, USA
Wednesday 7th December	Hot Club, Philadelphia, PA, USA *(matinee & evening shows)*
Friday 9th December	The Paradise, Boston, MA, USA *(matinee & evening shows)*
Saturday 10th December	The Paradise, Boston, MA, USA
Sunday 11th December	Oxford Ale House, New Haven, CT, USA
Tuesday 13th December	Bottom Line, New York, NY, USA *(matinee & evening shows)*
Wednesday 14th December	Bottom Line, New York, NY, USA *(matinee & evening shows)*
Thursday 15th December	Ukrainian National Home, New York, NY, USA
Friday 16th December	Stone Pony, Asbury Park, NJ, USA *(matinee & evening shows)*
Thursday 22nd December	Nashville Rooms, London, England
Friday 23rd December	Nashville Rooms, London, England
Saturday 24th December	Nashville Rooms, London, England

1978

Friday 20th January	Roundhouse, London, England,
Saturday 21st January	Darlington Inn, Camelford, England *Sue Barber's wedding reception*
Wednesday 25th January	Armadillo World Headquarters, Austin, TX, USA
Thursday 26th January	Fairmont Hotel, New Orleans, LA, USA *CBS Convention*
Friday 27th January	Opera House, Houston, TX, USA
Saturday 28th January	Faces, Dallas, TX, USA
Tuesday 31st January	River Days, St. Louis, MO, USA
Wednesday 1st February	Pogo's Kansas City, MO, USA
Saturday 4th February	University Of Colorado, Boulder, CO, USA
Tuesday 7th February	Zellerbach Auditorium, Berkeley, CA, USA
Wednesday 8th February	Coffee House, University Of California, Davis, CA, USA *(matinee & evening shows)*
Thursday 9th February	Lane County Civic Centre, Eugene, OR, USA
Friday 10th February	Paramount Northwest Theatre, Seattle, WA, USA
Saturday 11th February	Paramount Theatre, Portland, OR, USA
Tuesday 14th February	Jay's Longhorn Bar, Minneapolis, MN, USA
Wednesday 15th February	Centre Stage, Milwaukee, WI, USA
Friday 17th February	Kent State University, Kent, OH, USA
Saturday 18th February	Union Ballroom, Brockport, NY, USA
Sunday 19th February	Leona Theatre, Pittsburgh, PA, USA
Monday 20th February	Bogart's, Cincinnati, OH, USA *(matinee & evening shows)*
Wednesday 22nd February	Lehigh County Community College, Schnecksville, PA, USA
Thursday 23rd February	Rutgers University (The Ledge), New Brunswick, NJ, USA
Friday 24th February	Tower Theatre, Upper Darby, PA, USA
Saturday 25th February	Page Hall, Albany, NY, USA
Sunday 26th February	Brown University, Alumni Hall, Providence, RI, USA *(matinee & evening shows)*
Tuesday 28th February	Warner Theatre, Washington, DC, USA
Wednesday 1st March	University Of Massachusetts, Amherst, MA, USA
Thursday 2nd March	Quinnipiac College, Hamden, CT, USA
Friday 3rd March	C.W. Post, Brookville, NY, USA *(matinee & evening shows)*
Saturday 4th March	Moot Hall, State University Of New York, Buffalo, NY, USA *(matinee & evening shows)*

Monday 6th March	El Mocambo, Toronto, ON, Canada
Tuesday 7th March	El Mocambo, Toronto, ON, Canada
Thursday 16th March	Stella Cinema, Dublin, Ireland
Friday 17th March	Ulster Hall, Belfast, Northern Ireland
Sunday 19th March	Top Rank Suite, Cardiff, Wales
Monday 20th March	Odeon, Canterbury, England
Tuesday 21st March	De Montfort Hall, Leicester, England
Wednesday 22nd March	City Hall, Newcastle upon Tyne, England
Thursday 23rd March	Paramount Theatre, Asbury Park, NJ, USA *(cancelled)*
Friday 24th March	Eric's, Liverpool, England
Saturday 25th March	Eric's, Liverpool, England
Sunday 26th March	Locarno, Bristol, England
Monday 27th March	Winter Gardens, Malvern, England
Tuesday 28th March	Village Bowl, Bournemouth, England
Wednesday 29th March	Top Rank Suite, Brighton, England
Friday 31st March	Corn Exchange, Cambridge, England
Saturday 1st April	Sports Centre, Bracknell, England
Sunday 2nd April	Town Hall, Middlesbrough, England
Monday 3rd April	Tiffany's, Edinburgh, Scotland
Tuesday 4th April	Satellite City, Glasgow, Scotland
Wednesday 5th April	Top Rank Suite, Sheffield, England
Thursday 6th April	Rafters, Manchester, England
Friday 7th April	Rafters, Manchester, England
Sunday 9th April	Pavilion, Hemel Hempstead, England
Tuesday 11th April	The Garden, Penzance, England
Wednesday 12th April	Guildhall, Portsmouth, England
Thursday 13th April	Barbarella's, Birmingham, England
Friday 14th April	Barbarella's, Birmingham, England
Saturday 15th April	Roundhouse, London, England
Sunday 16th April	Roundhouse, London, England
Wednesday 19th April	State Theatre, Minneapolis, MN, USA
Thursday 20th April	Orpheum Theatre, Madison, WI, USA
Friday 21st April	Aragon Ballroom, Chicago, IL, USA
Saturday 22nd April	Music Theatre, Royal Oak, MI, USA *(matinee & evening shows)*
Tuesday 25th April	Shea's Buffalo Theatre, Buffalo, NY, USA
Thursday 27th April	Landmark Theatre, Syracuse, NY, USA
Saturday 29th April	Massey Hall, Toronto, ON, Canada *(matinee & evening shows)*
Sunday 30th April	Theatre St. Denis, Montreal, QC, Canada
Tuesday 2nd May	Music Hall, Cleveland, OH, USA
Thursday 4th May	Orpheum Theatre, Boston, MA, USA
Friday 5th May	Capitol Theatre, Passaic, NJ, USA
Saturday 6th May	Palladium, New York, NY, USA *(matinee & evening shows)*
Sunday 7th May	Leroy Theatre, Pawtucket, RI, USA
Tuesday 9th	Shaboo Inn, Willimantic, CT, USA
Wednesday 10th May	Chrysler Hall, Norfolk, VA, USA
Saturday 13th May	Seminole Jai-Alai Fronton, Orlando, FL, USA
Sunday 14th May	Jai-Alai Fronton, Tampa, FL, USA
Tuesday 16th May	Egyptian Ballroom, Atlanta, GA, USA
Wednesday 17th May	Wilson Auditorium, Cincinnati, OH, USA
Thursday 18th May	Circle Theatre, Indianapolis, IN, USA
Saturday 20th May	Uptown Theatre, Kansas City, MO, USA
Sunday 21st May	Cain's Ballroom, Tulsa, OK, USA
Monday 22nd May	Raul's, Austin, TX, USA
Tuesday 23rd May	Municipal Auditorium, Austin, TX, USA
Wednesday 24th May	Music Hall, Houston, TX, USA
Friday 26th May	Convention Centre Theatre, Dallas, TX, USA
Friday 26th May	The Old Warehouse, Dallas, TX, USA *Guest appearance at Delbert McClinton concert.*
Saturday 27th May	University Of Colorado, Boulder, CO, USA

Sunday 28th May	Music Hall, Tucson, AZ, USA
Monday 29th May	Symphony Hall, Phoenix, AZ, USA
Tuesday 30th May	Civic Auditorium, Santa Monica, CA, USA
Wednesday 31st May	Civic Theatre, San Diego, CA, USA
Thursday 1st June	Millikan High School, Long Beach, CA, USA
Friday 2nd June	Robertson Gym, Santa Barbara, CA, USA
Sunday 4th June	Hollywood High School, Los Angeles, CA, USA
Tuesday 6th June	Centre For The Performing Arts, San Jose, CA, USA
Wednesday 7th June	Winterland, San Francisco, CA, USA
Monday 12th June	Trinity College, May Ball, Cambridge, England
Friday 16th June	Ancienne Belgique, Brussels, Belgium
Sunday 18th June	Olympia, Paris, France
Monday 19th June	Volkshaus, Zurich, Switzerland
Tuesday 20th June	Schwabinger Bräu, Munich, West Germany
Thursday 22nd June	Theatre Carré, Amsterdam, Netherlands
Friday 23rd June	Congresgebouw, The Hague, Netherlands
Sunday 25th June	Orpheus Theatre, Apeldoorn, Netherlands
Monday 26th June	De Vereeniging, Nijmegen, Netherlands
Tuesday 27th June	Evenementenhal, Groningen, Netherlands
Wednesday 28th June	Audimax, Hamburg, West Germany
Thursday 29th June	Kant Kino, Berlin, West Germany (cancelled)
Friday 30th June	Neue Welt, Berlin, West Germany
Sunday 2nd July	Roskilde Festival, Roskilde, Denmark
Tuesday 4th July	Chateau Neuf, Oslo, Norway
Thursday 6th July	Folkets Park, Hunnebostrand, Sweden
Friday 7th July	Dad's Dancehall, Malmö, Sweden
Saturday 8th July	Masten, Kristianopel, Sweden
Sunday 9th July	Sundsta Aulan, Karlstad, Sweden
Monday 10th July	Konserthuset, Stockholm, Sweden
Tuesday 11th July	Folkets Park, Linköping, Sweden
Wednesday 12th July	Visfestivalen, Västervik, Sweden
Friday 14th July	Turku, Finland
Saturday 15th July	Tampsa, Karhula, Finland
Sunday 16th July	Kaivopuisto, Helsinki, Finland
Tuesday 25th July	Lone Star Café, New York, NY, USA
Saturday 23rd September	Grand Hotel, New Brighton, England,
Sunday 24th September	Brockwell Park, London, England (Rock Against Racism)
Wednesday 18th October	CBGB, New York, NY, USA
Sunday 29th October	Esby Gym, State College, Glassboro, NJ, USA
Thursday 2nd November	El Mocambo, Toronto, ON, Canada
Friday 3rd November	O'Keefe Centre, Toronto, ON, Canada *(matinee & evening shows)*
Saturday 4th November	Queen's University, Kingston, ON, Canada
Sunday 5th November	Algonquin College Gymnasium, Ottawa, ON, Canada
Monday 6th November	Alumni Hall, London, ON, Canada
Tuesday 7th November	Theatre St. Denis, Montreal, QC, Canada
Wednesday 8th November	Hamilton Place, Hamilton, ON, Canada
Friday 10th November	Canadian Lakehead Exhibition Coliseum Thunder Bay, ON, Canada
Saturday 11th November	Playhouse, Winnipeg, MB, Canada
Sunday 12th November	Saskatchewan Centre Of The Arts, Regina, SK, Canada
Monday 13th November	Saskatoon, SK, Canada
Tuesday 14th November	Northern Alberta Jubilee Auditorium, Edmonton, AB, Canada
Wednesday 15th November	Southern Alberta Jubilee Auditorium, Calgary, AB, Canada
Friday 17th November	Pacific Coliseum Concert Bowl, Vancouver, BC, Canada
Thursday 23rd November	Mido Hall, Osaka, Japan
Friday 24th November	Mido Hall, Osaka, Japan
Monday 27th November	Japanese Education Hall Tokyo, Japan
Tuesday 28th November	Japanese Education Hall Tokyo, Japan
Wednesday 29th November	Seibu Theatre, Tokyo, Japan
Thursday 30th November	Seibu Theatre, Tokyo, Japan

Sunday 3rd December	Regent Theatre, Sydney, Australia
Monday 4th December	Festival Hall, Brisbane, Australia
Wednesday 6th December	Canberra Theatre, Canberra, Australia
Saturday 9th December	Palais Theatre, Melbourne, Australia
Sunday 10th December	Concert Hall, Perth, Australia
Tuesday 12th December	Apollo Stadium, Adelaide, Australia
Monday 18th December	Dominion Theatre, London, England
Tuesday 19th December	Dominion Theatre, London, England
Wednesday 20th December	Dominion Theatre, London, England
Thursday 21st December	Dominion Theatre, London, England
Friday 22nd December	Dominion Theatre, London, England
Saturday 23rd December	Dominion Theatre, London, England
Sunday 24th December	Dominion Theatre, London, England
Wednesday 27th December	Top Rank Suite, Brighton, England
Thursday 28th December	Guildhall, Portsmouth, England
Friday 29th December	Pavilion, Bath, England
Saturday 30th December	Odeon Theatre, Canterbury, England
Sunday 31st December	New Theatre, Oxford, England

In-depth Series

The In-depth series was launched in March 2021 with four titles. Each book takes an in-depth look at an album; the history behind it; the story about its creation; the songs, as well as detailed discographies listing release variations around the world. The series will tackle albums that are considered to be classics amongst the fan bases, as well as some albums deemed to be "difficult" or controversial; shining new light on them, following reappraisal by the authors.

Titles to date:
Jethro Tull - Thick As A Brick   *978-1-912782-57-4*
Tears For Fears - The Hurting   *978-1-912782-58-1*
Kate Bush - The Kick Inside   *978-1-912782-59-8*
Deep Purple - Stormbringer   *978-1-912782-60-4*
Emerson Lake & Palmer - Pictures At An Exhibition 978-1-912782-67-3
Korn - Follow The Leader   978-1-912782-68-0
Elvis Costello - This Year's Model   978-1-912782-69-7
Kate Bush - The Dreaming   978-1-912782-70-3

Forthcoming:
Jethro Tull - Minstrel In The Gallery   978-1-912782-81-9
Deep Purple - Fireball   978-1-912782-82-6
Deep Purple - Slaves And Masters   978-1-912782-83-3
Talking Heads - Remain In Light
Jethro Tull - Heavy Horses
Rainbow - Straight Between The Eyes
The Stranglers - La Folie
Alice Cooper - Love It To Death